'There are so few people like Pastor Mick that this book deserves a shelf all to itself.'
Jeremy Vine, broadcaster and journalist

'The Duke and Duchess of Cambridge wanted to visit Pastor Mick to offer support and understand more about the work that takes place in Church on the Street.'
Ed Thomas, *BBC News*

'Mick Fleming's story is at the same time both unbelievable and real. It reveals a man who was dreadfully wronged and guilty of many wrongs – yet miraculously found forgiveness and the ability to forgive. Liberated from bitterness and guilt, Mick's response has been to do more good in one life time than a whole roomful of politicians. A gritty, gripping and moving book.'
Tim Farron, MP, leader of the Liberal Democrats, 2015–17

Pastor Mick Fleming has a degree in theology from the University of Manchester and was ordained in 2019. Three years later, he was consecrated Bishop of Church on the Street in Burnley and of The International Christian Church Network. Church on the Street is a Christian community dedicated to helping others, particularly those who find themselves homeless, struggle with addictions or are on the breadline. *Blown Away* has been translated into French and was published as *Rédemption: Du deal à la vraie Vie* by Mame in September 2023. A German edition is forthcoming in 2024.

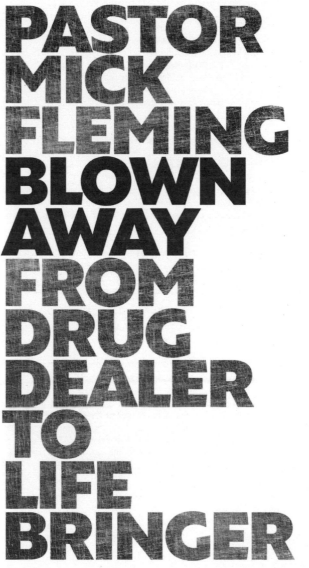

PASTOR MICK FLEMING
BLOWN AWAY
FROM DRUG DEALER TO LIFE BRINGER

spck

Originally published in hardback in Great Britain in 2022

SPCK
SPCK Group
Studio 101
The Record Hall
16–16A Baldwin's Gardens
London EC1N 7RJ
www.spckpublishing.co.uk

Reprinted once
Paperback edition published 2024

British Library Cataloguing-in-Publication Data
A catalogue record for this book is available from the British Library

ISBN 978–0–281–08665–8
eBook ISBN 978–0–281–08664–1

1 3 5 7 9 10 8 6 4 2

Typeset by Fakenham Prepress Solutions, Fakenham, Norfolk NR21 8NL
First printed in Great Britain by Clays Ltd

eBook by Fakenham Prepress Solutions, Fakenham, Norfolk NR21 8NL

Produced on paper from sustainable sources

For Kathleen and Gordon

Contents

List of plates

Credits

Photographs 1–16: The family's collection
Photographs 17–28: Phill Edwards – BBC

Foreword

It's impossible to visit Church on the Street and not be deeply moved by the work the organisation does for those in need. It is an extraordinary place that has been an important refuge and place of safety for so many. Often, it is only by sharing our problems and being honest with ourselves that we are able to heal and overcome life's challenges. And by doing so, we find just how deep the bonds we all share are.

HRH The Duke of Cambridge
July 2022

HRH The Duke of Cambridge became HRH The Prince of Wales on 9 September 2022.

1
FIFTY PENCE PIECE

BUZZERS RINGING. DOORS OPENING. A dark feeling deep down in the pit of my stomach. Policeman on the left, policeman on the right.

As the voices echo down the corridors that smell of disinfectant, I feel invisible. They speak to one another, but I'm not there. Then the final door. And in. The smell, the view, and the nurse with the pearly white teeth and the ruby red lips, who smiles and says, 'I'll take it from here, officers. Come with me, Michael, you've got your own room. But the door will be left open all the time, and don't worry, there'll be someone sat on the chair outside.'

I'm led into a room that . . . the bedding matches the curtains, the cupboard, the bedside cabinet. An institution.

My mind swirls like a kaleidoscope, but the colours just fall into grey as I wonder how. *How* has it come to this? Where's my rebellious streak? Where's the fight, the resolve that I had deep down inside me? How could I let the policemen just walk me in? Only weeks ago, they'd have had no chance!

No more power, just a sense of despair. Sinking into the bed and feeling physically pinned there as fear consumes me. My throat begins to get sore and dry inside as I remember what happened.

Why? How? And *what?* The memories start to flood back, and I long to escape the truth.

But here we are. Big powerful man with his head bowed. Lying on a bed in a psychiatric unit.

* * *

A bright, clear winter's morning. I come running down the stairs, late again for school, of course, and my sister presses a shiny, bright fifty pence piece into my hand. I love her; she's like a mother to me really. And a squeezy tight, 'Don't lose it!' I run out the house. No chance of me getting the bus! Keep the money, that was always my way.

I'm meandering and running and jumping, counting the squares on the pavement as I dance to school. A little boy with glasses and sandy curly hair, joy in his heart.

And a shortcut. Jump over the little river instead of crossing the bridge, off through the park. A big smile, life's good. I feel alive! I can smell, I can taste, I can hear.

Suddenly the sound switches off. Suddenly there's an arm around my neck and the taste of a woollen jumper in my mouth and all my eyes can see is graffiti on the wall and peeling paint on a seat and . . . I'm engulfed in confusion, afraid to cry, my heart thudding and thudding fit to burst. A strange smell, a dark aroma of sweat and sweetness, mixed together and blended. A pouting voice, and pain, like none I'd ever known . . .

In the corner I can see a bottle. For years and years afterwards, I imagined picking it up and smashing him around the head! But I never did. I was too afraid.

Thrown to the floor. My glasses broken, my knees bleeding. I'd become a victim.

I'd been raped.

His hand squeezed my throat. 'You speak a word of this, and I'll come and kill your parents! Do you understand?'

As I pulled my trousers up, I couldn't speak. But I looked at the face. I looked right into those eyes. I'd always remember that face. I'd carry it with me for a long time. No smile. Eyes of black. A tinge of alcohol on his breath. I'd never forget.

As I stumbled off, there were no colours any more. I couldn't see the sun. I couldn't smell or taste the air. It felt like my head had been plunged into a bucket of water. I sat in school, with everything going on around me and nothing going in.

Bleeding. Too afraid to even open my mouth.

'Fleming! Stop daydreaming!'

As the teacher shouted and the children laughed, I'd no smile to give. No conversation to offer. Everything had changed. A darkness fell over me. And it wasn't my choice.

I can't remember walking home from school. But one thing I know is, I didn't go that way. I took the other road.

As I looked down, I saw there was blood and a grazing to the palm of my hand in the shape of the fifty pence my sister had given me that morning – I must have squeezed it so tight. I'd remember later that Jesus character had holes in his hand. Well, so did I that day. But I also had one in my heart. And it wouldn't mend in three days.

Getting home, finding my bedroom, lying on the bed. Looking up at the ceiling and the patterns on the wallpaper. Trying to distract myself from what I was feeling. The corner of the cupboard sent a little shadow across the wall that looked like a tree. I was longing to see things that were normal and real.

But my world was upside down.

I tried to cry, but no tears came. There was a sensation in the pit of my stomach that hadn't been there before. Something that might be fear, but I wasn't sure. I really felt I should have fought harder. That I'd let myself down.

Night-time fell. The streetlamp outside was bright and shone through my curtains. I usually loved the way it danced on the wall. But tonight it looked different. Tonight his face was in the light as it moved around. Tonight I could hear noises in the trees as the breeze blew outside, and I was scared. 'I'll kill 'em, if you tell anybody!' echoed in my mind. I bit the pillow as hard as I could as the tears finally came, and for hours and hours I sobbed. But nobody heard my cries. Nobody was there to comfort me. I was alone.

A new day. I opened the curtains and looked out. The world was grey. Not blue. Not bright. A Saturday morning, the TV downstairs, the smell of bacon cooking, and me on the top landing.

As I came down, the door opened. My dad. Stumbling, his face stricken, his voice cracking with emotion, and those awful, dreadful words that echoed round the house: 'Your sister's dead!'

Stunned silence. Then a sound I've heard many times over the years; a sound like no other in the world. The primeval scream of a mother who's just lost a child. A sound of pure love and pure pain. It bounced off the walls and hit me like a body blow. And I knew. I could never speak of the day before. Sobs and wailing and cries, and this grown man, my dad – my hero – reduced to tears. But no room for me as he comforted his wife. No space for me.

I began the long walk back up the stairs, my legs so heavy . . .

Mum and Dad's room. And there, Mum's painkillers. The tablets she took so she could live a life with her back pain. Quick! A sachet. Back to my bedroom. A handful, swallowed. Lay down . . . And a calmness fell over me. I felt as if I was floating on a cloud. I felt angels had lifted me up on high! I could see colours again. I was safe; I was warm. As I lay there, the bed seemed to wrap itself around my body to comfort me. Maybe I'd found God! I just floated away. There was no pain. Reality had gone. I was at peace.

And then a terrible, terrible fall, like dropping from the sky and hitting the bed, so hard. Such a come down. It wasn't a dream. The nightmare was real, and it was only beginning . . .

I became a drug addict that day. Chasing the peace – seeking something, *anything*, to take me away from the reality and pain of who I really was.

'God help me,' I cried out. 'If you're real, *help me!*'

And the answer came instantly.

Silence.

My god was a drug, a tablet, a drink, glue, as I progressed through the ranks of addiction. The little boy with the glasses was gone. The sweet child with the fifty pence that he grabbed so tightly . . . I looked at the hole in my hand, and I felt the pain.

I was done with fear. No one was going to hurt me again.

2
DEAL DONE

THE CURTAINS WERE CLOSED in the siting room. It was really cold, because the radiator had been turned off, and we were told not to go in there. But we could see dimly through the patterned glass doors that divided it from the dining room.

A knock at the door, and they brought her in. Ann. My beautiful sister, in a box. Shadowy figures removing the lid and standing it up in a corner.

Still no tears from me. I looked at my mum and I could see something in her eyes, something new. She didn't know what to think, what to say, who to be – *what* to be. She was stunned. My dad, bewildered, but rushing round trying to comfort people. I noticed that nobody was sat close like we used to be. My sisters there, but not there. One on the floor; one on the pouffe; Mum on the settee; Dad on the chair. There were gaps between us all. And those gaps would be there for a long time.

My dad slid open the doors and walked into the front room on his own. He had some rosary beads in his hand, and he leant over the coffin and spoke words I didn't really understand. When he came out, my mum went in and reached towards my sister. And said nothing.

Then she came and took me by the hand. Hesitating, but curious, I followed. I peered in . . . it was like my sister, but not like my sister. Her face just wasn't the same.

I said to my dad later, 'It's not her.'

'It is, son.' He put his hand on my shoulder. 'It is.'

I remember the earrings she was wearing, gold dangling at the side . . . her hair wasn't as she'd worn it. I wanted to shout REALLY LOUD! I wanted to put life back into her! But she was gone. Lying in that beautiful coffin, so smooth to the touch . . . And on the lid, a name and a date, etched into the brass.

Etched into my heart.

Something broke that day. We didn't grieve together as a family – we all seemed to go our separate ways. Shortly after, my dad, being a good Catholic man at the time, invited people round from the church. Into that cold room they went – men in suits, with shiny shoes. People I never knew, had never met, with stern faces, bowed heads, holding their rosary beads. They encircled the coffin and began a strange chanting sound, praying to a God who was far, far away. To me, it didn't sound human. To me it felt like a demonic force had invaded the room, pouring out emptiness . . . And poor Mum, sitting on the other side of the glass doors, trying to be normal and becoming more unhinged hour by hour, with two young children to look after – and myself. Lost.

* * *

The noise became too much and I went upstairs to my bedroom. Sat on the bed while the chants seemed to get heavier and heavier, louder and louder, until it was almost hypnotic. I began to feel as if I couldn't breathe and I started to panic . . . I couldn't stand it any more. I hit my head against the wall and still the sound got louder and louder. I hit my head again, but it just wouldn't stop!

There were tablets in the room next door. In I went. A handful again. The desired effect . . . lie down and wait for the warmth. Let it wrap itself around you and just float away . . .

The noise and the prayers got quieter as I calmed down. In my imagination, I saw myself smiling. It felt wonderful. I looked at the lightbulb and it glowed. And then it started to change colours – a multicoloured lightbulb, like a rainbow! I felt a great joy as I fell into a warm, deep, comfortable sleep.

Time passed, until I was woken by one of my sisters coming into my room. One of the young ones.

'You're not dead, are you, Mick?'

'No, love. I'm just having a rest.'

It was like she knew. She *knew*. As she left the room, I wondered if it would be a good idea for me to die as well . . . How would I do it? Maybe if you take a lot of painkillers, and then just go to sleep, the real peace will come? Anything's got to be better than the pain.

But something inside me just wouldn't run with it.

I was trying to make the tablets last. I knew in the end I'd be caught, though I was kind of hoping Mum might just think she'd lost them. Because her mind wasn't with it. Manipulation and deception – an art that would become my stock-in-trade.

The chanting had stopped, and the stern-faced men with suits and shiny shoes had gone. I went downstairs and found my dad and my uncle sitting with the coffin. They were drinking Jameson's Irish whiskey, as though we were traditional Irish people. Dad offered me a glass, and while he poured, my uncle told me, 'Sip it, lad. Don't put anything in it. Just drink it.'

I raised the glass to my lips. My body shook a little. And it tasted . . . foul! It tasted horrible! But it soothed that painful feeling in my throat as it went right down into my stomach. And I could feel its warmth.

That night I learnt how to use alcohol to numb my pain. Something that would blight my life for the next thirty years.

* * *

The black car pulled up outside. People lined the streets. All the men took their hats off as we drove by. And inside, the wonderful smell of that cream leather trim, the feel of the mahogany wood inlay under my fingers . . . Anything, *anything* to distract me from the reality of what was happening.

Another crowd outside as we entered the church and processed up the aisle behind the coffin. We were the centre of attention, the congregation all looking at us, as if we were . . . TV stars! I couldn't *stand* it. I looked away, up to the really high roof with its strange bright emblems. I looked at the priest doing the service in his fine, colourful gown, as he stood in front of something like a little house – a tabernacle. He spoke about my sister, although he didn't know her. Somebody read a little piece from the Bible that none of us understood. And then they sang a song: 'I've called you by your name; you are mine. Do not be afraid.' I looked around and people had tears running down their cheeks. But not me. All my crying was done.

I looked at the priest and I wanted to spit at him. I looked at my mum and my dad and I just felt disdain. I looked around me in that packed church, and I felt hate inside for every one of the people standing there. The *power* of that feeling was very strong. And I realized in that moment that drugs and drink and hate were close friends. And on the days when I didn't have a drink or a drug, I always had the anger. And I got comfort from that.

Later, we stood at the graveside and they lowered my sister in a box into a hole in the ground. People threw soil in, weeping and sighing, but in my mind I was punching, hitting, kicking . . .

I walked out of that cemetery a different person. My grieving was done. The little boy was buried with his sister, and I made a decision. I was going to cause havoc. I was going to run wild. I was going to give my life over to the evil side. And on the journey home in the car, I began to smile.

Home. Running upstairs to rip off the horrible, hideous clothes and tie that reminded me of the week I'd just lived out and hated. There was nothing gentle left in me. I looked in the mirror and I saw my face. And when I smiled this time, there was something different . . . I looked more like the man who'd hurt me. My eyes were black and I began to laugh. 'Heh, heh, heh, heh, heh!'

As you read on, you'll find a story of evil, frustration, deceit . . . and then a fall – a fall so low it found me in that psychiatric unit, wondering where and why and how. But for now I had a mission. And my mission was to destroy. And to take.

The next few weeks saw me putting a jacket over the back of the chair in my bedroom and practising stealing a wallet out of the pocket. I'd think about the things I could pinch from the shop. I'd walk in, count how many seconds it took the shopkeeper to come out to the front, devise a plan, draw it out and then execute it. Nobody knew. I had this great power. I was *good* at being bad. By the time I was thirteen I had a lot of money. I'd buy things for my friends but never tell anyone how I managed it. It was my secret.

I see now that some time over the next twelve months or so I stepped into a fantasy world. My mind created something that wasn't real. I remember watching *The Godfather* on TV and being fascinated. I knew that I too had the heart to hurt.

My first act of violence happened just outside the school gates. The boy was bigger and older, and he began to bully and push and prod at me. But I had something he didn't have. I had a spirit of death deep within me. I felt it rising from the pit of my stomach, down my arms into my fists, and then blackness and darkness as I punched each punch, getting faster and faster, and blood – all over me. But not mine. People pulling me off, girls crying, 'Stop, Mick! Stop! Stop! That's enough!'

But it wasn't enough. It was never enough for me. He wasn't going to get back up. As I stamped on his face, people began to look away. The cheers of 'fight!' started to fade. I'd gone too far. I couldn't breathe. But I loved it. The hairs on the back of my neck stood up. I *loved* it! It was like a drug – it made me feel untouchable. I licked my hands and tasted the blood, and felt as if I'd done a deal with the devil. Nothing could touch me now. Nothing would ever stop me.

People began to take notice. I'd stepped into a new life. A new world. A new beginning.

3
RUBY LIPS

THE NURSE WITH THE RUBY LIPS bobbed her head round the door.

'Come on, Mick! I'll show you where the tea and coffee is, and you can help yourself.'

As I followed, I noticed she was very attractive. She smiled, she oozed empathy and she liked me, though there was no sexual feeling there. *What a foolish woman*, I thought. *You come too close, and I'll tie you in knots.*

She pointed out where the tea and coffee and kettle were – I could help myself to a brew any time I wanted. Left there at the counter, I looked around and saw people at different tables, subdued, heads bowed – people who were ill. But I wasn't like that, surely? I wasn't one of them.

We were on the third floor, and through the window I could see right across the town. That was my world out there. But I was in here.

I made a coffee and the old rebellious streak began to return – I could feel it. My fingers started tingling, my mind started running quickly. The feeling in the pit of my stomach was oozy but nice! As if something was about to happen. My eyes fell on those green sachets of coffee. There's no one watching. Hand in the jar. Sachets in my pocket. And retreat. Back to my room.

I'd had a thought. I opened the coffee sachets . . . lined them up on my bedside cabinet. Fished for my wallet and a card to crush the powder, then I racked it up like lines of cocaine. I took my last dirty five pound note and rolled it up. I could feel the excitement building, the adrenalin in my stomach. I was back! I was rising above all the problems, all the things that had pulled me down. I could start all over again. I felt fresh. I felt new.

My hands began to shake and a little bead of sweat dripped on to the cabinet as I put the note to my nose and sniffed. One line. The other nostril. Another line. And then pause for a moment . . . and yeah! I'm sure I can feel something . . . I'm sure I can! And just as I bent back down to devour the third line, ruby lips walked into the room.

Her soft brown eyes looked at me like a mother looks at a struggling child. 'Mick, what *are* you doing?'

'I just need something to lift me out of this. I just need drugs – you won't give me anything!'

'Mick, it's decaf!'

Her ruby lips curled and I smiled myself for the first time. We both had a little laugh, a little snigger.

'Throw it away, Mick. It's for drinking, not for sniffing.'

That morning, sitting on the bed, I lost something. This mighty man, who thought so highly of himself, in a psychiatric unit, sniffing decaf coffee, thinking he still had it going on. The reality of where I was and what I'd become was beginning to sink in. And I felt afraid. And when I feel fear, I become dangerous.

I walked out of the room and looked around. *Yeah*, I thought, *I could take anybody in here.* I checked out the staff – *Yeah, even them.* But I was feeling uncomfortable, and at lunchtime I stole a knife and hid it under my bed. Actually, it was a butter knife. I failed to understand there was no way

I could sharpen it up, and you definitely can't butter people to death! So it was pointless, and they found it anyway when they searched my room.

The episode underlined the fact that I was ill. But also a threat. After years of having weapons, I felt naked without one. I didn't want to lose a knife, a gun, anything. In a moment of madness, I snapped a credit card in half and sharpened it when I could. Hid it in my sock. If needed, I could stripe someone. That made me feel safer. After all, I'm in a place where people are not quite right in the head. Unlike me . . .

'Medicine time. Medication.'

This should be interesting! What delights have they got on offer? I like the different-coloured pills and the liquids they're pouring out. And sure enough, one shot of green liquid for me. I couldn't wait . . . Took it and lay on my bed, and the world became woozy once more. I drifted out of my body, floated high on the clouds and imagined myself wrapped in a rainbow, being comforted, feeling free . . . That wonderful sensation of rest always seemed like love to me. But it wasn't real. I knew I'd have to wake up tomorrow and face the world as it truly was. I couldn't get pearly white, ruby lips out of my mind. It wasn't sexual; her eyes just had something different. She was a woman who cared. But why should she care for someone like me? I was confused as I drifted into a deep sleep. Tomorrow would be another day to reflect on my life. Another day in a psychiatric unit with people who, I was beginning to realize, were just like me.

Lost.

* * *

Sitting alone on the ward with a coffee. People all around, but they're finding my demeanour intimidating. I was so envious of those who had visitors. Nobody had come to see me. I'd burnt every bridge – with my children, my wife, my father, my sisters and even my friends. Then, in the corner, I noticed a strange-looking elderly gentleman. Another *smiler*. He didn't seem intimidated. He was only small and I could have crushed him with one hand. But he wasn't afraid.

As he shuffled over, I noticed the laces of his brown shoes were tied just perfectly, exactly the same way. Very smart. Wearing a suit, and a jacket over the top. Old school.

'What's your name?'

'Mick. If it matters.'

'Well, it certainly does matter, young man; it certainly does matter. I'm Arthur.'

'Pleased to meet you, Arthur. I've got nothing to say, Arthur, really.'

'Can I talk to you?'

'You can, Arthur. If you must.'

Arthur was the kind of guy I've never understood. He spent his free time going round hospitals, talking to people who had no visitors. You know, the sad, lonely ones. The ones that life's given up on.

Yeah, it seemed Arthur came to see people like me. It didn't feel very nice.

He put his hand in his pocket, and you won't believe what he brought out. A bag of toffees.

Give me strength! I've got an old fella, with sweeties, sitting in front of me at a table in a psychiatric unit. What on earth?

But he just said one thing: 'Tell me now. What happened to put you in here?'

And as I paused and looked at him, he pushed his spectacles up the bridge of his nose. He really wanted to know.

'Hang on a minute,' he said. 'Let's get us a brew first.' And off he went. Came back with two coffees. Fresh ones. I'm sure they were decaf but who cares? They tasted a lot better.

'Tell me, son, please. I need to know.'

'Arthur, I'll tell you something if you tell me something,' because I was thinking, *Is he undercover? Is he police?* I'd a strange notion in my head that if I looked around the ward and saw people wearing white training shoes, they were undercover policemen. My illness was deep, my paranoia was massive. But Arthur had nice brown shiny shoes, tied the same way. He couldn't be undercover. That made perfect sense to me.

He told me the story of his son, who'd taken his own life. And I think he wanted to cry, but it was so long ago . . . You could see the lines around his eyes. He'd done all his crying, but he never forgot. And as we sat there, it began to feel as if I could be Arthur's son. It felt like I had a father speaking to me. Arthur looked like my dad.

I began to see what I'd done. I began to know what I'd done. I began to feel so sad.

Arthur just pushed the white bag of sweets forward. 'Go on, go on, go on. Take two, take two!'

So I did. One for now and one for later. Into my shirt pocket it went.

'Come on then, son. Spill the beans. How does somebody like you end up here? What happened?'

The story I'm about to tell moves me to tears. It's a story of destruction, yet from it came love. It's a story that put me in a psychiatric unit, but it was the *beginning* of change.

'Arthur, I wasn't a very nice man and I'm still not. My life's been wrecked by addiction and crime, and I've hurt so many people. Do you really want to hear what I've got to say?'

'Yes, I really do.'

We moved from the table and sat on the comfy sofas, far from anyone else.

And so began the story of my unravelling . . .

I found myself in a car in the early hours of the morning. A job. Debts had to be collected. People had to pay. I was smoking crack heavily, as I always did, and nothing felt any different that day.

A gun, wrapped in a carrier bag. Wrapped up nice and tight. And on the journey, there was nothing new, nothing fresh. Sometimes collecting a debt is about the collecting rather than the debt. People's pride, you see, just won't let other people get away with anything.

My journey was quick. I was on my own. I knew where I was going and I knew exactly what I was going to do.

I pulled up early in the carpark outside the gym. I could see the lights inside. I could hear the sounds, the clangs, the bangs of heavy weights falling on the floor. And I waited. I waited patiently. One more cigarette. As I lit it, I blew the smoke out the window. I was thinking about my family, but I didn't feel anything. I'd become very cold. Very cold indeed. It seemed as if I had no emotion. And no fear.

Then the bright red door swung wide and out he walked. I grabbed the gun and began to open the car door, but just then he turned his back and took the hands of two little girls. Both blonde. One on either side. That meant nothing to me. I didn't care.

I approached, the gun at my side and evil in my heart, and then something, something miraculous . . . A brightness shining from the hands of the children where he was holding them – such a brightness! The light hit me in the eyes; it blinded me! I couldn't see!

Ten, fifteen seconds maybe.

Of utter devastation.

I felt ill. I staggered back and put one hand on the bonnet, leant there for a moment, took a deep breath. They'd walk by. But the gun! They couldn't see that. I jumped back in the car. I couldn't breathe. My eyes began to stream, water pouring out, and I started to sweat. My heart beat faster and faster and faster, and then I began to be sick. My stomach ripped – I felt the sheer physical sensation. Blood was coming up. It was all over the car; it was all over my clothes. I looked like I'd been stabbed or been in a massacre. There was blood everywhere, and snot and . . . tears, yeah, maybe even tears.

I had no idea what was going on.

I threw the gun on the passenger seat. 'Nice and slow, Michael. Drive nice and slow like nothing's wrong. Follow every rule and break no law.'

So I drove away calmly, but inside, my head was pounding, my brain was spinning. What on earth was happening to me? I turned into a little industrial park and pulled up. No one around. It was quiet but the music was on. And what was playing? Johnny Cash, 'The Man in Black'. And that was who I was: a man in black. Without goodness or respect or decency.

I prayed that day. In that moment, I cried out to God: 'God, if you're real, you'd better help me!' It was a demand more than a prayer. And the prayer was answered fast . . .

Silence.

Utter silence.

I punched the stereo. I began to thump and headbutt the steering wheel. Now there's blood dripping from my hand. My head's in turmoil, whizzing faster and faster and faster . . . My breathing's getting shallower and shallower, and I feel like I'm having a panic attack. I've no crack on me but I've got vodka. I unscrew the lid as blood drips on to the bottle. And I sip it, and then I swig it, and then I smash it down into my mouth as quickly as I possibly can. That burning feeling, that nice burning feeling . . . ahhhh.

But it's not worked. It's not slowing me down, and I've had it, I've just had enough. Even the God who loves can't love the unlovable! And in that moment, I grab the gun . . .

Put it under my chin.

And pull the trigger.

Deadly silence for one second.

It didn't fire.

I dropped the gun on the floor and began to weep. I hadn't cried properly for thirty years and my body was utterly wracked. I felt I might never stop. Is there a God? Was my prayer answered? I knew that gun. It didn't misfire. It couldn't! The very nature of the weapon wouldn't allow it.

It *must* be a miracle.

I looked around the car and . . . some mints. I pushed one into my mouth. I could barely taste it. Mint and vodka and blood, all mixed together.

What had just happened? What had just happened to *me*? Was this God real? He didn't seem as distant . . .

I drove away, knowing that I had to get rid of the gun and the car in the usual way. But before I put the gun to bed, I fired it three times in a field. It didn't misfire. Had there been light from the children's hands? Had there been a real miracle? Did God love *even me*?

I wish I could say that I never used drugs again. That I never drank again. But I did. That very same day, I was smoking crack and drinking vodka. Later on, though, in my flat, something in my head seemed different, something in my thinking seemed different. As I left the house the next morning, I took a deep breath, looked down the long tarmac drive and hoped for a future.

Then they pounced!

Police from every direction.

I was pinned to the floor, cuffed and dragged away. A struggle, a cell and then an interview room – answering questions I invented in my head. They'd ask about criminal acts, I'd talk about sausages; they'd ask about firearms, I'd talk about goldfish. They could never trip you up if you were insane. *Was* I insane, or was I just pretending? I didn't know, but I certainly wasn't going to tell them anything. Especially the CID man, in his white trainers.

Then the tone of the conversation changed.

'Would you like a cup of coffee, Michael?'

'It's Mick!'

'Would you like a coffee, Mick?'

'Thank you. Yes.'

'Would you like a cigarette?'

Hang on a minute! Good cop, bad cop – they think I'm stupid.

'Come on, we'll take you for a cigarette.'

And they did.

And then back. And more questions. And more crazy answers.

'Where were you last Thursday?'

'Do you believe there are giraffes on the planet Jupiter?' Not exactly what they wanted to hear.

Slowly but surely I began to feel something unusual was going on here. What was this change in tactics? I'd been in so many police interviews, but none like this.

They left me sitting there. And when they returned, they had a doctor with them. It soon became apparent to the doctor and to the police that I needed some help. I was dangerous. To the public. And to myself.

The police were kind as they helped me into a nice comfy car. There were three of them: one driving and two in the back with me. During the journey, they chatted about the night out they'd had, about their kids – about life! I was invisible. I simply wasn't there. Such a strange feeling.

When we arrived at the hospital, they took me out the car, one on either side and one remaining in the driver's seat, and walked me up to the door. Then I did begin to feel afraid.

'Can I have a cigarette before we go in?'

'We don't have time, Mick.'

'Then I'm not going in.'

I smoked that last cigarette. I knew I had nowhere to run, nowhere to hide.

What would become of me now?

* * *

'You see, Arthur, I've always been no good.'

Arthur looked at me strangely, and as I glanced at his face I saw that he had a tear in his eye. He reached over and touched my hand. Not quite holding it, just resting his on top.

'You know, Mick, God is with you. And he has great plans for you.'

I felt the impact of what he was saying. I didn't want it to be true, but I *felt* it.

'*Great* plans for you, Mick.'

'Thank you.'

As Arthur stood up and shuffled away, I wondered: was there really a God? *Did* he have plans – for *me*? How could that even be, with everything that I'd done?

I looked around the unit and for the first time in many years I really saw people. In the corner was a young lad with a shaved head, who appeared poorly. His mother beside him seemed heavy, desperate. I looked to the left and there was another young lad on his own, with curly hair, who'd just drifted. His body was there but he wasn't. And on my right, I saw this bloke about my age with grey hair. He was shaking. I knew he was an alcoholic. I knew it just by looking at him, and I felt a connection.

Maybe there was hope?

Maybe this was just where I was meant to be?

4
TRIO

NIGHT-TIME CAME. Lots of noise. Bells ringing, buzzers going. Takeaways being delivered and the smell of fish and chips. People returning after a cigarette, but they wouldn't let me go out!

That old rebellious streak that just didn't seem to want to leave. I'd no cigarettes anyway.

But in the corner – always in the corner; why is he always in the corner? – sits that one person you just know, you just know they *know*.

I take a sip of coffee and make eye contact. Grey hair, and something in his face, something in the lines that scream out, *I'm like you*.

Expensive shirt with a beautifully starched collar. Unbuttoned, two buttons down. A pen in his top pocket. Hands shaking – I recognize that shake, I recognize it well. He approaches and sits down and begins to speak. Like me, he's an alcoholic. He's an addict. We understand each other.

'Do you need a fag?'

'I do, but they won't let me go out.'

'Then take these. I'm sure you know what to do with them.'

He offered me a full packet of cigarettes – for free! He put them in my hand, then gave me his lighter.

Off to the toilet and . . . aaahhh, the joy! My head dizzy, spinning around, I didn't care if there was the smell of smoke. No smoking on the ward indeed! Not for me, not for people like us. We take our pleasures wherever we go. Two cigarettes later, the place is absolutely stinking.

And as I leave, a male nurse approaches. He puffs out his chest: 'Lighter?'

'No thanks, I don't need one.' I walk past. If he tries to stop me . . . That wonderful old feeling I thought had gone would build up inside me and explode as I shoved him back. But I could see in his face that he wasn't up to the task. He just didn't fancy it. And he backed off.

I felt empowered, and that power seemed to be about adrenalin. It seemed to be about destroying anything that got in my way. Yet I always seemed to hate myself afterwards. I didn't want to be a bully.

I sat back down and you could hear the feet of the chair scraping on the floor as I pulled it closer to the man who'd given me the cigarettes. 'How long have you been in here?' I asked.

'I've been in two weeks. I'm an alcoholic, you see.'

'Yeah. So am I.'

'Really? You?'

The stories we went into; the tales we told; the sharing of ourselves with each other.

And then, a very special moment. He looked me right in the face. I could see the lines underneath his eyes – and the bags. His hands were still shaking. He opened his mouth and his lips started to move, but it was like I wasn't comprehending what he was saying; it was like my head was back under water. There were noises coming out, but I just couldn't quite grasp . . .

'He abused me. It went on for years and years.'

I heard these words . . . *I heard these words!*

And my ears were opened. A grown man, a man like me – it had happened to him!

I stopped him. I said, 'Tell me again.'

He told me a tragic story of how his father would systematically abuse him in the worst way possible. And I thought, *Nobody has ever told me anything like this before. I thought I was on my own.*

Yet as he continued talking, I began to wonder if there might be a way out. We were victims, but was there any possibility we might eventually become survivors?

Another slurp of coffee and I found tears running down my face. I was so touched and shaken by what he'd said, I could hardly contain myself.

'And what about you, Mick?'

'It's the same story but not as bad.'

'Don't say that. It's always as bad, whether it happens once or a thousand times.'

'Yeah, maybe, maybe . . .'

He carried on telling me about his life and what he did now. It was as if a book had opened up. Pages were turning and although I couldn't read the writing, I could see the pictures. And the pictures were in technicolour! So vivid.

You see, he was a thief. He was a prolific shoplifter. But not just any shoplifter; he was a *successful* shoplifter. He got organized, he dressed well, he went out and committed crime . . .

I was slavering. I was loving it. I needed another cigarette. Can't I just smoke it at the table? Maybe I will!

'No, no, no, Mick. Go to the toilet.'

Off I went, another cigarette, and back. More! More! The next episode of the drama, please!

As he spoke and revealed who and what he was, I felt a connection like I'd never felt before.

Several days later, when I had a ten pound note, I ripped it in half. I gave him half, and I kept half. I wish I could tell you in that second why I did it. I just felt I wanted to share something. And that's all I had of any value.

Half a ten pound note.

The price of a friendship.

Money well spent.

The nights on the ward would never be the same again. There'd be chats and talks and bonding and other people joining in and . . . that's when we met him. Sat round a table. Another one. The trio was complete.

Shaven head. Tattoos, but not very nice ones – letters and dots and symbols all over his hands – and a strange look in his eyes. Dark eyes, yet light dancing in them nonetheless. And as our conversations joined together, three in one – another victim, repeat victim, multiple victims – my new friend got up and punched the wall, seven or eight times. Then came and sat back down.

'Why do you do that?'

'The voices tell me. If I do it they go quiet, and if I don't they get louder. Do you hear any voices, Mick?'

I stopped and thought for a minute. 'Yeah, I do.'

My other friend: 'And what do they say, Mick?'

I beckoned them nearer and they pulled in close. The tension was tight and high . . . the expectation . . . the serious looks.

'What do they say, Mick? Tell us!'

And then in one spontaneous moment: 'DIE! That's what my voices say to me. Die! It's like something wants me dead, even against my will.'

My friend with the alcohol problem: 'I think that every day, but I don't hear it.'

And my other friend: 'Shall we chuck the tables up and throw the chairs out of the window?'

'No, no, no, it's okay, brother; it's okay. Stay calm.'

'Yeah, but it'd be fun!'

Part of me wants to do it, but the other part just *really* wants to help him.

'Mick, why are you wearing pants with holes in?'

'Well, because I don't have any more.'

And then it happened. My new friends got up, and after a little while they came back, bearing gifts. New training shoes. A new tracksuit. A little bit of money.

I felt an emotion inside me that I really didn't understand. I felt as if wanted to cry! But it wouldn't look good if I did. Why were they giving me stuff? I hadn't threatened them; I hadn't intimidated them; I hadn't forced them to do anything.

They just did.

Should I accept? Well, they weren't wearing white trainers, so they definitely weren't under cover!

In truth we were three victims, sitting round a table, sharing what we were but also what we had. And something seemed to happen when we told the truth. It was like we were one.

If there was a God, and I was wondering about that more and more, he was with us round that table. Because when I'd sat down, I had nothing but old rags of clothes and no proper shoes for my feet. But when I stood up, I had a full outfit.

* * *

For the next few days, I thought deeply about my new friendships, and that prompted me to think about my relationships outside – in the real world. And they weren't like this. For the first time in my life, I felt that I fitted. I felt I belonged. I'd finally found . . . my people. How might that change things? I didn't know – I really didn't know at all.

One day, not long after this, there are buzzers and alarms going off again, but this time screams too, shouting and banging. I hurry in to see my friend with the tattoos, and he's shaking, no light in his eyes, nothing dancing in them. He's made tracks all over his arms and across his throat – you can see how deep they are, and there's blood everywhere, dripping and running . . .

He was so poorly, so ill.

He'd started to copy my behaviour and talk a little bit like me.

And he'd spoken to ruby lips – and misunderstood. He thought she loved him; that she would whisk him away and marry him. The razor blade was the only way out.

My heart felt so sad, yet I'd only known him a short time. I was a man who couldn't care less about people, who could harm and hurt people, but I went back to my bed and cried. I would miss him, and everything had changed again.

The three victims were now two.

My alcoholic friend was desperate. He was taking medication to stop him rattling from the alcohol withdrawal. And

I needed a drink. I managed to get someone to go out to buy some drugs, *any* drugs, and a bottle of gin.

In came the merchandise: quart of gin, nice green bottle. What drugs had he got me?

Aagh! A big lump of phet – not my drug at all. Didn't really like the sensation, but hey ho . . . What if I take it all and then drink the bottle of gin? What will happen then? Will the vision of my friend's open, gaping wounds with all the blood running down, go away? Will it relieve the pain? If it does, I'll carry on taking drugs and drinking for the rest of my life.

'How's that, God?'

No answer.

God seems to be eerily quiet when I want to do bad things. I've always noticed that. He never says, 'Mick, just don't.' He never seems to speak to me . . .

My friend needs a drink. I open the bottle and give it to him first, but he only takes two swigs and says, 'No, I don't want to do it, mate! I'm detox, I don't want to do it. I'm all right – no more for me. Thank you.'

So I eat a massive amount of amphetamine and drink the bottle of gin. All of it, down in one. And wait.

Lying in my room, my heart begins to race . . . I start to feel sick. My head's spinning, and the heat, the fever that comes over me . . . I'm starting to shake. Ten minutes . . . fifteen minutes . . . an hour. I can't get off the bed.

One of the male nurses pops his head in. 'Everything all right, Mick?'

'Yeah . . . yeah.'

He must know . . . he *must know* what I've done. Surely everyone can see!

I'm stuck. I'm trapped. I feel like someone's glued me to the bedcovers. I pray, 'God! Take this feeling away – this is horrendous!' I've never felt like this when I've taken drugs before. I'll never take phet again!

And the agony *won't go*. As ill as I feel, this is going to go on all night.

That was the last time I ever had a drink. Or ever took a drug. They didn't take away the feelings – or the picture of the gaping holes and wounds and blood.

So I'd have to find another way . . . another way to live.

* * *

Sitting up late one night, and there's a young boy, in his twenties – very intelligent and a really lovely lad. You know: if your daughter was going out with him, you'd be pretty pleased.

'Why are you in here?' I ask.

'I just want to die.'

'Why?' I'm thinking he's so young, he's a good-looking kid, he must have everything going for him. He doesn't look as if he even drinks! 'Why do you want to die?'

'I just want some peace, mate.'

'Peace from what?'

He started to tell me about how he smoked weed, lots and lots of weed. And he couldn't stop. Before, he'd felt all right, but now he had a mental illness that took him really deep – his thoughts were so deep. As we chatted into the early hours of the morning, I found his notion of life after death was different from mine. His was, it's like you've just turned the TV off. And it's black. And there's nothing.

He craved nothingness.

But that wasn't what I wanted! That wasn't what I believed. That wasn't what I thought, deep down inside. I wanted light. I wanted real light. I wanted to feel. To be warmed, to be comforted. I wanted it to be real. I didn't want the light turning off. I wanted a new life . . . I wanted to be in the peace!

As we talked over the next few weeks, it became obvious that his craving for death was far greater than mine had ever been. He was lost in this darkness that whirled around in his head and wrapped itself around his thinking.

One day I saw his father. Many years later, in a strange twist, he and I would become friends and now we work together at Church on the Street. But back then he was just desperately trying to care for a beloved son, and feeling helpless and powerless.

The lad told me that he was in hospital because he'd made multiple attempts to kill himself. Over and over and over again. Such was his craving for darkness. I tried to convince him that, surely, light was better than darkness, because if you have light, there is no darkness.

'Darkness comes at night,' he'd say. 'Turn off the TV; there's nothing . . . stillness . . . nothingness . . .'

'What if you're wrong?'

'I'm not.'

Six months after we left the psychiatric unit, this wonderful, highly intelligent young man took his own life. All my words, my hopes and aspirations for him came to nothing. Maybe the world was just too much for him. Good people do die. Spiritually and mentally, some of us are more ill than others.

He was so young that I'd felt a little as if I was his dad. I'd try to protect him on the ward and speak up for him. He was definitely lost. Yet such a lovely human being.

* * *

After several months on the ward, I wasn't on suicide watch any more. I could come and go as I pleased, so I'd take myself outside the door for a cigarette. But then I'd find I couldn't go any further and it began to worry me. Surely I wasn't becoming institutionalized? It's true, I felt comfortable in my new surroundings; I felt like I belonged.

Then one day, when I was sitting on a bench in the fresh air smoking a cigarette, it dawned on me that a reluctance to face up to my outside relationships might just be related to my reluctance to move around freely outside.

And I realized that my children, my father, my wife – all the mistakes I'd made . . . It was me. *It was me!* It was the things I'd done that had led to my own downfall.

I thought about my first wife and what I'd put her through. I thought about all the times – when the children were only babies – that the front door had been kicked in and the police had raided the house. I thought about the drugs and the guns and the money that she knew of but chose not to see. I thought about how I must have manipulated and controlled her, and I wished it could have been different. I wished I could just have been nice.

One day she woke up very poorly. Her mind had been so distorted and twisted that she'd had a complete breakdown. She was diagnosed with bipolar disorder, and I used to visit her on the very next ward to where I was sitting. I became a single parent with an addiction, and I really wasn't very well myself. Maybe that was why I'd found it so difficult to separate the person my wife was from her illness. I treated her badly, and for that I'm truly, truly sorry.

You see, our relationship wasn't the kind I had with my two friends in the psychiatric unit. We were all equal; we were all there for the good of one another. I'd never had a relationship like that with anyone before. When I thought of my children, they were mine – everything was mine, mine, mine; me, me, me!

I flipped my fag on to the floor, lit another one straight away, and as I smoked I thought of my second wife, who'd had another child with me. I'd manipulated and kept the truth away from her too, hid my addiction, hid the things I was doing. I felt so sad, so alone. I knew I'd lost her now. Two beautiful women had cared for me, but I just hadn't understood how to give. I'd never known how to show love. Or to receive it back.

Relationships are truly tough when you have to be . . . somebody else.

5
FATHER JIMMY

A NEW DAY. I've got used to where I am. I've got used to where I'm living. I *daren't* think about the future, and I don't want to go back to what I was before, so I'm not making too many plans.

The male nurse calls me in. 'Mick, I've got drug and alcohol services coming. What do you think?'

'Why? What are you using?'

He looks at me. 'What are you talking about? It's for you!'

'No, I'm all right, mate. I'm all right.'

I was so much in denial, so arrogant, that I thought he was talking about himself and asking me for advice. Oh dear! As I look back . . .

The appointment's set and I've got a meeting. They're coming to see me 'on outreach'. It's something, I suppose.

Two of them. I sat down and enjoyed the conversation because I got to talk all about me. I told them anything and everything they wanted to know and then signed up for drug and alcohol services. When I left the unit, they'd try their best to help me.

One of the guys had something different about him – a peacefulness. I wondered if he was another one of those Christians, those God-botherers. Always fascinated me. Were they weak? They'd a strange sense of not having fear, so they couldn't be. I had to admit that whatever they had, it was attractive.

It turned out the lad was a Christian pastor who was volunteering for drug and alcohol services. This was his first outreach and I was his first ever client. And I know (because he told me many years later) that he prayed for me. He said I was the most poorly person he'd ever seen. I thought I was all right!

You see, when you're truly mentally ill, you don't know the depths of it. In the car on the way to the unit, the conversation between him and his friend had been that I was a very, very dangerous man. I wasn't to be on my own with anybody; the nurses had to be there and they couldn't let me off the ward. He's since said to me, 'But I wasn't afraid, Mick. I just wasn't afraid.'

He's also told me that he always knew God would be with me. It was becoming a theme. I thought back to Arthur touching my hand and saying, 'God's surely with you, Mick.' I didn't really get it. To be honest, I wanted there to be a God. But I didn't feel him. I couldn't . . . *grasp* him.

A nun used to come in and bring communion, and being a good Catholic boy (brought up by nuns who would hit me with sticks and tell me Jesus loved me) I thought, *Well, it can't do any harm. I'll go and see the lady and she'll give me communion.* Not the wine, unfortunately; just the host, just the bread. She seemed quite nice. She'd touch my cheeks and she looked as if she really liked poorly people.

I couldn't wait for the visit each Sunday. For fifteen minutes or so, you were in a room with her by yourself. She'd give you communion, and then she'd pray for you and talk to you, and . . .

At last, I got some peace. My head seemed to slow down completely when I was sitting with that lovely, kind nun. I once asked her about the devil and if she thought he was real. She did, and when I heard her say that, my mind swirled and curdled, almost as if it was shutting down, and I was transported back in time . . .

'Mick, I need a lift, I need a lift! Take me over. I'll put petrol in. I need to go over to Liverpool.'

'Okay – what for?'

'I need to move some furniture for a priest friend of mine. Father Jimmy. Lovely fella.'

'All right, Dad. I'm not doing anything.'

And off we went to this village just outside Liverpool. When we walked through Father Jimmy's door, I encountered the smallest man I've ever seen. Yet he had a presence, a spirit, about him far greater than his stature. Dark hair, Irish, Scouse-type of accent, and just full of love. He smiled. 'Yeah, come in. Yeah, sit down. Yeah, all right.'

There's another man there in a suit. A biggish fellow. Nicely spoken, softly spoken.

Father Jimmy makes us a brew. Nice cup of tea, just how I like it hot, sweet and the colour of tar. And as I'm sipping at this tea and thinking, *Where's the furniture?*, Father Jimmy says, 'I want to pray for you.'

I feel really uncomfortable. My dad's sort of aware of what might happen. He knows Father Jimmy and his friend, and he knows me. I can be a bit of a handful. I wear a T-shirt. I'm a big lad, well trained up, proud of it, flexing my muscles even in front of two priests.

So my dad leaves. And they begin to pray.

I'm not kidding you, they tried to do an exorcism on me!

And listen, there was salt, there was oil, there was all sorts of stuff set out. And I couldn't stop laughing. Until I got really angry.

They just kept praying, and I got angrier and angrier. I started to swear and they just kept praying. I started to kick and spit. I toppled the settee over. I threw the coffee table to one side and the hot drinks splattered all over the wall. And they just kept praying . . .

Until a huge, foul SCREAM that felt as if it came, not from my lungs but from the pit of my stomach. It burst out of my mouth. It was piercing, like a scream and a whistle together. You just wanted to put your hands over your ears! And I ripped my T-shirt – ripped it off. Then I fell to my knees. I couldn't move. And still they just kept praying. Praying, praying . . .

Possibly after an hour or so things came to an end. I seem to remember one of them putting oil on my forehead, though it's all very vague and shadowy now. But something did happen and I did feel different when I left. It was as if I could breathe properly again – in and out, in and out. I felt really good. I felt happy.

On the drive home, my dad seemed not cocky exactly but confident that my life would be completely changed. He smiled and talked and called me son, and put his hand on my shoulder, and I *felt* like a son. I felt like a son should feel.

But the minute I got back, I reached out for a crack pipe and a drink. And the old feelings returned.

* * *

As I become aware of the nun again, she asks, 'What do *you* think? Is the devil real?'

And I say, 'If he is, he's been a close friend of mine for nigh on thirty years.'

'Let me pray for you, Mick. And God bless you.'

The only nun I've ever met who didn't want to hit me. I knew she really felt sorry for me and maybe, just maybe, if she'd said, 'Jesus loves you,' I wouldn't have asked why. But she never did. She never did.

Time passed quite slowly in the psychiatric unit, because I didn't go anywhere. I was afraid and my pride was so great that I couldn't bear to let people see me this way. I remember one of the cleaners coming in, someone who knew my family, and hiding in the corner so she wouldn't spot me. Of course, being one of those nosey busybodies, she came over to ask how I was doing. I couldn't help it. I just exploded, 'Fuck off!'

The ward stopped dead as she turned away. I felt bad. I did want to change! I wanted it so badly. I knew I was going to have to try and put the past right. I knew if I carried on the way I'd been going, my life would be pretty short.

The pain was great but the longer I spent in that unit, the more hope I felt. I thought that if Jesus was real, if the stories about him were true, then he went through the pain. He didn't swerve it. In my estimation at the time, human beings tried to avoid pain at all costs. They drank, took drugs, slept with loads of partners, ate lots of things – did anything rather than feel what they were feeling. But you can't avoid pain. Bad things happen; people die. And if the Jesus story is real, he went through the pain and then rose from the dead! Just *maybe*, if I can go through this pain, and if I ask him to go through it with me, *maybe* I'll come out to new life too. *Maybe* there's a chance!

I wasn't sure. I'd had people say to me, 'Jesus died for your sins,' and I'd wondered, *Why would he? And what does that mean anyway?*

And then I had a thought. Imagine all the crimes I've committed, everything bad I've done wrong – and that's a lot, that's a heck of a lot – and there's this bloke, and everybody's robbing him, knocking him to the floor, kicking him in the face, spitting at him, jumping on him – he's going to die! And he's being battered for all the stuff I've done. All he needs to say is, 'It wasn't me – it was Mick!' and the beating will stop. And he will live. But he doesn't grass! He just takes it! He dies for all my crimes. I'm not a grass, but I'm not going to die for anyone else. Not even for a good person, never mind a bad one like me.

I wonder if that's what it means for Jesus to be on a cross. He took it for me.

Or maybe I'm just making things up in my head. I do that sometimes. Especially when I'm trying to get some comfort.

Who is Jesus? Can he get me out of this psychiatric unit? Can he help me get back on my feet? Can he forgive me?

Because if God's real, I can't forgive myself.

And I never will.

* * *

I remember standing looking out the window. The rain was banging on it, making a nice noise, a comforting noise. The little bubbles of water all over the pane meant that everything outside looked misted, and I felt that was exactly how I'd been seeing for the last thirty years – all bubbly and misted.

That rainy day seemed like every other day. I'd become accustomed to my environment. I wasn't scared of anything or anybody when I was in the unit; my fear seemed to have moved to the outside world. And as I sat there drinking a comforting cup of coffee, my thinking cleared and I began to realize that I was clean! I was actually clean and had been for a few months. And I was sober! I felt shocked and a little bit proud of myself. No rehab. I hadn't even considered it. I'd no desire at all for drugs or drink.

Yet I knew I wasn't properly well. I still had a massive amount of emotion inside me. Some days I felt as if there was a car battery in the pit of my stomach; on others, that I was carrying a heavy load on my shoulders. And I didn't know what to do with what was burdening me.

I did recognize that I felt a deep sadness that my marriage was over and there was nothing I could do to save it. I'd sent my wife many text messages and she bounced them all straight back at me. At first I thought her phone must be broken. Then, slowly but surely, it dawned on me that she was telling me we were done. It felt like a stab in the heart.

My pride said, 'I'm really poorly. Look at me, I'm here in hospital and you won't even help me!' But the truth was, she just couldn't take any more. The deceit, the drugs, the never really knowing me . . . It must have been such a crushing blow to find out the truth.

Where would I go? What would I do? And what would become of me?

I'd no answers, but the coffee was good, the biscuits were even better, and I was here. I'd accepted my lot – for now.

* * *

I noticed the door open and in came a very slim, very tall man. Probably one of the tallest men I've ever seen – he wasn't far off the ceiling! Flat cap. Glasses. Very poorly – you could tell by the way he walked. I always know how somebody is by the way they walk.

He began to pace, up and down, backwards and forwards, like a tiger in a cage. He was in the wrong environment and, as he walked around, I knew the adrenalin had begun building, because I've been him. He walks and he walks and I've got my eye on him, but then just for a split second he disappears and I feel something tight around my neck, pulling and choking and transporting me back . . . and I'm that child again and all I can see is the bottle in the corner, and d'you know, this time, *this time*, I have the courage . . .

It didn't end well for him.

Or me. Violence wasn't the answer.

I picked up something and hit him with it, freeing myself, and the staff were running round and alarms were going off – all the things that I kind of liked really, the drama of life, with me at the centre.

He lay bleeding on the floor.

I didn't resist when the staff pushed me off into my bedroom and told me to stay there. A couple of hours later, when I came out and a new shift had begun, it seemed as if everything was all right. He wasn't there; I think they'd moved him somewhere else. It was as if there were going to be no consequences.

That was fine with me. I didn't do consequences. I didn't face things. I always manipulated and shifted and shirt-changed and moved. Nothing would happen.

Until the next day, when there was a meeting of the doctors and nurses and me. And this was the outcome.

'Mick, you've done really well in here. I don't think there's much more we can do for you, and keeping you in here in this environment is only going to make you more poorly. So it's time for you to leave.'

Time for you to leave. Time for you to leave. *Time for you to leave!*

I could feel my face distorting with fear. I didn't know whether to cry or laugh or just get angry. I thought about maybe beating the doctor up so they'd never let me out. But I didn't. I accepted it. I had to go tomorrow.

I went to the nurse and said, 'I've nowhere to live. Can you help me?' It was probably one of the first times in my life that I'd ever asked for help. I got a place that day in a homeless hostel.

In the morning, as I said goodbye to my friends, I breathed in deeply. I wanted to take the smell of the place with me. I didn't want to leave. Craving to stay in a psychiatric unit might seem a strange thing to many people. But remember, this was the first time in my life I'd ever had friends. True friends. It was the first time in my life I'd ever felt as if I fitted in. And now I was having to leave it all behind and step once more back into a cruel world. Yes, I was different – I was clean. But how long would I last?

I left with a carrier bag containing everything I owned in the world. Forty-two years of age. A homeless man. In a homeless hostel. In my home town.

* * *

I was shown to my room and it was really nice, with a bed and curtains – different from the hospital, more homely somehow. There was a mirror on the wall, a sideboard-type table for writing and eating on, and a microwave. Wonderfully, I'd a shower room with a bath and my own toilet. It all seemed good. But I was feeling really bad . . .

About twenty minutes later, a knock came on the door and a young lady took me down to the office. I wandered in and introduced myself to the four staff there, who were all very nice and polite. Then they turned back to their computers and their writing pads and carried on with their work.

This lady was my keyworker. Big yellow-gold earrings, nice smile! But very thin eyebrows, very thin . . .

Over the past few months, as I'd begun really noticing people's faces, I'd found that when I looked into their eyes I could often see something. I felt like there'd been a sadness in this lady's life and that maybe this job wasn't just a job? Maybe there was something from the past that had prompted her to do the work she was doing. Anyway, she helped me fill in all the forms that were necessary and she supported me. I don't think I'd have got through my time in the homeless hostel without that lady with the earrings. Again, she was very attractive. She specially smelt lovely!

But there was nothing sexual. This was quite new to me – women who could just be friends with you, or who you could talk to like people. Quite a shock.

The first night, lying in bed with the fresh smell of clean covers, felt a little bit like having my own place. But I missed my friends. I missed the routine. And the meals and . . . What would I eat now? What would I drink? What *time* would I eat? Would I have to buy my food?

I had no money. How would I survive?

All these thoughts whirling round in my mind. And just at the point I was about to fall asleep, I needed a cigarette.

Out the room, down the stairs. Two flights to the front door. Sat on the step, smoking a cigarette. It was almost like I'd swapped one institution for another.

But this time I could choose.

This time I was clean.

I could smell the strong reek of cannabis. I could hear the noise of people drinking and laughing. It would be so easy, so easy just to pick up a drink. One swig would take away all the anxiety that was wracking me. But I knew the relief wouldn't last.

So, as I sat on that step with my cigarette, I said a little prayer. 'Jesus, *please* . . . help me to go through the pain.' It hurt so much, even saying it. 'And help me come out the other side to new life.'

That day, I began to live on a more spiritual basis. Only in my words. But it was a beginning.

I'd made a beginning.

6
THE VISITATION

I'M SITTING IN THE OFFICE talking to lady earrings, wondering how much money I get on this benefit thing – how wonderful it might be, how rich I might become . . .

And when I hear, it's like I've just been hit around the face with a wet fish. She tells me it will be £90. And I should get it within the next couple of days. My face! My jaw just dropped and she definitely saw the disappointment. Well, you couldn't miss it. I could feel my fist clench and I felt *so angry*.

'How does anyone manage on £90 a week??'

Her face changed too. Her head dropped. The earrings swung back and forth. 'Mick, it's £90 a fortnight.'

No reply. No answer. Just, 'Thank you. It's going to be a struggle.'

I left the office. And I was wondering again about the God thing. I'd noticed that whenever I tried to pray, I always said 'In Jesus' name' at the end. It felt as if I was praying to Jesus. And I kind of thought now would be a good time to pray. So I said, 'You know, Jesus, just kind of help me? I know you've never really helped me before, but I'm asking you to help me now.'

And then I had this thought. I wondered if God had been there all along. And he had been helping me but I was just too blind to see it. I began to think again about the past, and I recalled the time when I'd pulled off the motorway and I was driving down a slip road in the early hours of the morning.

The traffic lights turned red, so I stopped, pulled a cigarette out and lit it, turned the radio up just a touch . . . and then, a sudden squeaking and squealing of tyres as a car braked heavily alongside me. My window was down and I could smell the rubber. I looked to my right and in a split second, a noise like a whip being cracked, three times in quick succession. No bang! Not really an echo – just three cracks.

I'd been shot at.

From no further away than four feet.

And all three shots had missed.

Two had gone through the window and out the other side, and one had gone into the door panel. I felt the breeze rippling across my legs.

I had no fear. I was completely calm, and I remember catching a little glimpse of my eyes in the mirror and they were dark. I laughed – a deep horrible throaty laugh – because I'd seen the face of the man with the gun and I knew who he was. And they knew I knew. In that moment, they fled through the red light. There was no traffic and I followed.

The hunted had become the hunter.

I lost them, but I remembered that incident, held it in my mind, folded it up and tucked it away into a safe place for a later date. No fear. Nothing. Coldness. Like it didn't matter. I'd always expected to die anyway. I'd seen that much death, even as a kid – at sixteen, seventeen, my two best friends had died in quick succession. Death didn't seem to faze me; it just seemed inevitable.

I wondered now, had God been there on the slip road? Had he kept me alive? And I thought about those people I'd met on the ward, saying: 'God's surely with you, Mick.'

Was he?

I tried to make sense of how God might reveal himself. I thought of those I knew who went to church and I couldn't see that they were special. I couldn't see that they lived their lives any differently. And I wondered again, is Jesus real after all?

I recalled when I married my first wife and we didn't have much; how she'd have to hide behind the settee with the kids if someone came to ask for money. And a thought came to me: just imagine spending your whole life, because you're in debt, hiding behind the settee, urging the kids, 'Be quiet! Be quiet! Be quiet! Pretend we're not in!', and they're banging on the door and shouting through the letterbox, 'We know you're in there!'

Hiding in the dark, not turning the lights on, all your life. Until one day you answer the door by mistake, and it's Jesus! *It had been him knocking all along!* He'd been calling you to tell you he'd paid off your debt. You owed nothing. And you've wasted all those years, pretending there's no one home. When all along Jesus was calling you to open your heart – to him.

But I didn't know how to open my heart. I just couldn't do it. I didn't know what to do. So for now, I'd just keep praying and asking.

The day came when my big fat £90 whizzed through the letterbox! What would I do with this massive amount of money? Tobacco, first thing! Then I thought, *I need a suit.*

I spent every penny I had on a nice suit, a nice white shirt, a thin black tie and some shiny shoes. Then I got dressed up just to walk around town. Just to let people see. *Look at me! I look smart. I'm back!*

Trouble is, I couldn't even convince myself it was true, never mind anybody else. I just felt . . . sick – yet with a nice suit. All the things I'd done in the past to help me bounce back and pull myself together availed nothing. Shiny suits, shiny shoes . . . I didn't know what I was going to do now. But I'd keep praying, 'cause the suit certainly wasn't working!

Two days later, I was in the middle of one of my prayer sessions. Praying was all I had, though most of the time I felt I was just speaking to myself and saying 'Thank you, Jesus' at the end. In fact, I was beginning to wonder if I shouldn't be back in that psychiatric unit! I was having conversations with someone I couldn't see, who wasn't answering back, yet I'd keep on talking regardless! Perhaps I had some vague sense that I was getting to know 'him' or 'it' . . .

I sat there on my bed saying, 'Come on, Jesus, give us a squeeze. I don't know what's happening to me. I've got this fantastic suit – don't know why I bought it – I've got a load of baccy. But I've got no money, I've got nothing to eat, nothing's fixing me. Maybe you've been keeping me alive all these years because everybody else is dead. I've been shot at, people have turned up to kill me – it's happened over and over and over again. I even tried to kill myself, and that didn't work! Jesus, is that you?'

Silence.

No answers.

I wonder and wonder about Jesus. I keep thinking he's real in my head, but he seems to be *quiet* when I speak to him. He never seems to say anything, and then . . . I remember.

When I was sitting in that car, when I pulled the trigger, the answer came later. Ahhh! Maybe I'll just wait and see. Maybe I'll just give it time. I've asked the question. Now I'm going to leave it to you, Jesus – see what you think.

* * *

I'd begun training at the gym. I was getting fitter, healthier and stronger. Felt pretty lonely though.

Still, after the meeting I'd had in the psychiatric unit, I felt obliged to go to drug and alcohol services, and there I was assigned my very own drug and alcohol worker. *Woopey do!* I thought.

In the first meeting, we sat down and he said to me, 'You're such a nice lad, Mick. Why didn't you just stop?'

I couldn't believe what I was hearing. 'Just stop?! Hey, listen mate, you've got the answer to life itself: just stop. Have you ever had diarrhoea?'

'Yeah.'

'Just stop!'

A deadly silence. A little smile on his face, though, I must admit. But I didn't have any confidence in him. Anyway, he tested me for drugs, for alcohol. I was quite confident because I knew I hadn't used anything. And I came back clean.

'There's an abstinence programme that you can go on – a counselling, emotional attachment programme. It's group therapy and it's very good, Mick. You don't have to go away to do it; you can do it in the community. You'd just come here. We have a professional counsellor and it takes twelve weeks. What do you think?'

Well, I didn't have anything to lose. Why not?

Over the next few days, I hammered the gym. I wanted to look good in this new situation. I'd be meeting new people, making new friends. I felt nervous, I had butterflies, but I was praying. I wasn't doing much, but I was praying! And in one prayer, I asked, 'Jesus . . . is it you who's always been looking after me? And what should I do next? What should I do?'

When I prayed, I would keep my eyes shut, but I always had to open them before I finished. Just in case anyone was around watching me, or someone walked into the room, because, you know, I didn't want to look a fool. I didn't want people to think I was a nutter. I've just come out of a psychiatric unit and I'm in a homeless hostel; I've just spent all my money on a suit instead of food, but God forbid they think I'm a nutter!

Anyway, on that day I opened my eyes as normal before I'd finished praying. And there at the bottom of the bed was a bright, white light.

You can work out for yourself whether you believe what I'm about to tell you was a manifestation of my illness or whether you think it was real. It doesn't matter to me because I know what I believe! And Jesus works in people's illnesses anyway.

So back to the bright light at the bottom of the bed. I stared; I couldn't speak; I watched it get brighter and brighter, clearer and clearer . . .

At the bottom of the bed, in my room in the homeless hostel, was an angel.

That's right. An angel. Seven or eight feet tall. I know what you must be thinking. So was I at the time! *Mick, you're losing the plot.* But I'd never actually *seen* anything before;

I'd never had any kind of vision, ever. I wanted to touch it, though that might have been a bit rude really . . . I thought, *I'll speak to it.*

So I went, 'All right, mate?'

And the angel went, 'Yeah, I'm all right, pal. How are you?'

I guess that's how angels talk – or mine did!

'What do you want? What are you here for? And are you real?'

'Yeah, I'm real.'

'What do you want?'

'God sent me. Got a message for you, pal.'

'All right, let's hear it; I've been praying for that – let's have it!'

'He wants you to go and stand against a brick wall in the middle of the town centre at exactly seven o'clock.' And he told me which wall. It's about two minutes away from the homeless hostel.

'Why?'

'Just go. Will you do it? Yes or no?'

'Yes.'

'Right, catch you later – I'm coming back. But not now. See you later.'

'All right, see you later. What do I call you?'

Gone. *I guess I'll just call him Angel!*

I made myself a coffee and pulled out a couple of custard creams, dipped them in, burnt my fingers, got that sugary-sweet taste in my mouth, because I thought, *Either my blood sugar's low, or I'm pretty poorly.*

But it seemed so real! Seven o'clock. Against a brick wall. In the middle of the town centre. Not five past, not five to – has to be seven o'clock. Got to be there for seven.

As the time clicked on, I thought, *Yeah, I'll go.* Then, *NO, I'm not going!* I'm toing and froing. I feel like a ship being tossed about in a storm on the sea. You know – bounced around, looking for some calm water but there's none to be had. I'm in the middle of the storm and I can't get out of it. I didn't really know what to do. I wanted to take a chance, because I prayed for God to speak to me and show me a way. Answer some questions for me. I couldn't avoid going, really.

So that's what I did. It got to a quarter to seven. I rolled a couple of fags, stuck my lighter in my pocket and off I went.

Next thing, I'm leaning against the wall, with one foot raised, the other on the ground, and setting fire to my cigarette. As I smoke, I'm thinking, *Oh God, nobody else knows what's going on here! They're probably wondering, Why's that crazy fella leant against that wall?*

''Cause an angel told him to.'

I don't think that would go down very well. Can you imagine if the police had come and I'd told them that? I think I'd have been in the car with a nice man, straight back to the psychiatric unit.

I can see the town hall clock, it's so close. It's five to seven and the clock's ticking . . . and I'm really having doubts. What was I doing here? Why had I just . . . what was *wrong* with me?

There was no one else around. It's really quiet. And I'm randomly leaning against a wall. I throw my cigarette on the ground and stub it out with my foot, slowly, because I think I want to hang on a bit longer. Just in case, you know . . . just in case.

The town hall clock bongs and chimes seven o'clock. And just as I'm about to leave, a man walks round the corner and puts his hand out. 'All right, Mick? I bet you didn't expect to see me here, did you?'

I shook his hand as my jaw hit the floor. For two seconds I couldn't speak.

'Come on in, I've got the keys. It's anonymous. I'll make you a brew.'

'What?' A million things went through my mind. Does he know the angel? How did he know I'd be here? What . . .

It turned out he was one of the guys from the office in the homeless hostel, one of the people who were always tapping into a computer. I didn't know his name, but he was one of them!

He took me in, made me a coffee. Other people began to arrive and we sat round in a circle.

It turned out that it was a narcotics anonymous meeting, a twelve-step programme to help people like me who suffer from addiction and problems in life.

I was stunned. They were all talking about God and higher powers, and I'd been sent there by an angel. I wanted to shout out, 'Guess why I came here!' Then I thought, *Better not. Not quite time yet. I don't think I'm ready to say that, and they're surely not ready to hear it!* But it was true. How? Was this God? Was I deluded? Or was it real?

You see, over the years, I've noticed that with all the miracles I've witnessed, some of which will be documented in this book, the supernatural is just normal; it's the timing that's crucial. And this was good timing. It was miraculous.

After the meeting, I felt as if I had hope. I felt as if I could start all over again. I felt there was something that could guide me – and I called it Jesus. They called it lots of different things, but my higher power would be Jesus.

He'd sent me an angel and I don't think he'd sent them an angel!

And that's what I got out of that meeting – Jesus is my God. And I'm going to follow him and pursue him, just like other people do. Let's see what happens.

I went back home and smoked many, many cigarettes. I tended to think better when I smoked and that's why I smoked a lot. And drank a lot of coffee. Those things that kept me awake, even though I wanted to sleep. Just another trait that I'd struggle with over the years.

The angel had said he'd come back. And sure enough, he did. The day after. He appeared in exactly the same way. I prayed, opened my eyes and, while I was still praying, the light got brighter and there he was!

I'd so many questions, so much to say. 'Angel, guess what! You'll never guess what's happened!' And I kind of stopped and thought, *Yeah, you probably already know what's happened, don't you, seeing as who probably sent you.*

'Anyway, what do I do now?'

The angel said something that really troubled me, and I went from real excitement to real disappointment. *Real* disappointment. 'Jesus wants you to forgive the man who hurt you . . . when you were a little boy.'

'I can't! I don't want to. And I can't.' You see, I'd fantasized for years about cutting his throat, about stabbing him, about how I'd torture him, what I'd do to him . . . It made me salivate when I thought about it, I got so excited. I *couldn't* forgive him!

'Jesus wants you to do it. He'll show you how. And if you do what he asks, he wants you to go out and tell everyone you meet about him. And it will go all around the world.'

Well, I didn't know anything about Jesus really. Except that he sends angels. He stops you getting shot when you're in cars. You stick guns under your chin and they don't go off.

So he *saves* you really? Yeah, Jesus saves people like me. I'll have that! I do know something about Jesus. And I can tell others he saves people. Especially bad people.

Oh no! Even bad people like *him*?

Does Jesus save people who smell of sweat and sweet stuff, people with tinges of alcohol on their breath, people who squeeze children's throats and say, 'You tell anyone about this and I'll kill your mum and dad! Do you hear me?'?

DOES JESUS SAVE PEOPLE LIKE THAT?

I don't want to tell people about that Jesus. I don't care where he wants to send me. I'm not doing it. I can't do it. I *won't* do it!

Will I?

* * *

Everything the angel had said was miraculous, but so troubling – so difficult to take in. I tried to tell myself that my mind had just made it up. But the more I did that, the more real it became. I had been there – in real time. It wasn't a dream. I really didn't understand.

I felt I didn't want to forgive, and that I was quite justified in that. But I felt troubled too. What the angel said wouldn't leave me for a long time. It remained in my mind, and I thought about it almost every night before I fell asleep. It wasn't painful – it was really challenging. This wonderful God, this wonderful angel . . . but they wanted me to do something that seemed impossible.

Nonetheless, my life had started to come together a bit. I was going to the gym. I had my NA meetings. I was building my relationship with Jesus through the people I was talking and listening to. I wasn't as afraid and, as I started my abstinence programme with drug and alcohol services, I made some wonderful friends.

There was one in particular – we ended up like brothers. He was a smaller version of me: thick-set, stocky, just not as tall. He'd had a life like I had. He'd lost a brother; I'd lost a sister. We sort of understood each other really well. He started training with me at the gym.

And, before long, I began to build a relationship back with my dad. This was bizarre, because sadly, and to my shame as I say it now, I was the kind of guy who went to visit his dad when he was in a hospital bed with cancer and spat in his face and told him I hoped he'd die.

You see, I blamed Dad for my mum dying. Of course, it had nothing to do with him; she died of natural causes. But I had all this anger inside me that I wanted to take out on someone, and he was the nearest. I'd also robbed my dad of lots and lots of money over the years of my addiction.

He'd forgiven me.

He was in his eighties by this time, but he'd always kept himself fit and the three of us would train together. I loved it. I was building relationships like I'd never had. And after the gym, me and mini me would tootle off, back to our programme. It was helping us be more clear-sighted about the things we'd been attached to, yet it was highly emotional. There were around fifteen of us, men and women mixed together in a small room, and plenty of tears, anger and frustration. The counsellor was a great guy.

He was very gifted at pulling things out of people, pushing and prodding and using the group to help facilitate that work.

It was in one of these group sessions that I had my last exceptional, violent outburst. I think the counsellor made a mistake, but it worked well – in the long run. He had all my notes and knew that I'd been abused. He put an empty chair in front of me and moved everyone to the side. Then he asked me who was sitting in the chair. And I couldn't speak. I started to get angry, but only slowly. I wasn't fighting it; it just wasn't happening as quickly as normal.

'What do you want to say to him, Mick? Tell him! Tell him what you want to say to him!'

The anger started to build. The hairs on the back of my neck rose, even my knee joints tingled. My knuckles clenched, there was burning inside my fists. My hands felt so heavy, almost like sledgehammers. My body was relaxed but massively tense at the same time. I had pins and needles running through my head, right down my back.

'Speak to him. Tell him.'

I turned and saw a pen on the table. I grabbed the pen. I stabbed the chair. I attacked it. I smashed it to pieces. I spat on it. I ripped the chair apart! I punched the wall – went right through the plasterboard! There were screams and echoes, alarms and banging . . . women and men in the group running out.

It probably lasted only three or four minutes. But afterwards, a scene of devastation. As I turned, I saw the counsellor petrified in his chair. My eyes were open wide, staring forward. 'Who's next?'

'Breathe, Michael; just breathe!'

And I did. I followed his instructions. I breathed. I started to calm down and come back to earth. Mini me came alongside and put his arms around me. We fell to our knees and shed a few tears together. He had his problems, he'd had a past; he understood.

I left something behind in that room. The counsellor had taken a risk, but I remembered the angel talking about timing . . . perhaps the timing had been exactly right.

The day after, I had a feeling inside. I want to say it was humility, but I didn't really know what humility felt like then, to be honest. It was a bit painful, but it felt all right. Maybe it was to do with not being so much in control? It wasn't a joyful, singing and dancing, jump-up-and-down feeling, but it was all right. I remember going to the gym that morning and training with my dad and mini me, and it was . . . all right.

As time went on, with all the support I was getting from the homeless hostel and the NA sessions and the new people I was meeting, I started to begin to live a new kind of life – one based on sobriety. I was constantly thinking about my new pal Jesus. He still didn't mean everything, but he meant something – because my life was changing, and though I didn't know what would become of me, I thought it would be all right.

Maybe that's all faith is: it's going to be all right. I've got Jesus.

I finished the rehabilitation course and got a certificate. I felt quite proud because it was the first time I'd had a certificate since I swam two lengths at about six years old! I don't know where it's gone now. I've not been very good over the years at keeping things like that. But it felt good. What was even better was that my dad and two of my sisters came to watch me graduate. My sisters . . . I'd robbed them, I'd caused absolute mayhem and turmoil, I'd called them every name, and they came to support me! They even spoke, and when one said, 'I feel like I've got my brother back!' there was a tear in my eye. I knew the path I was on now was different and it would not be easy. But it was doable – it was doable.

I'd lined up a role volunteering, helping people just like me who were struggling with addictions and alcohol problems, who were homeless, who were mentally ill. I had something to give and felt as if I was good at it! I always asked Jesus to help those I prayed for, and he always did.

The difficult thing about working with people in that world, as I still do today, is that many, many die. And sure enough, mini me – he couldn't handle the pressure. He relapsed and subsequently took his own life.

I've seen so much death. So much pain. With mini me, though, it felt as if the pain wasn't mine to carry. I could be sad and that was okay. I could pray for him and I did.

Over the years, most of the fifteen people who were in that group have passed away.

But I had an angel.

And I'm alive.

7
MAD MICK

EVEN AS A MAN, I was a mummy's boy. I remember one time when I'd been out all night, and the police had been to the house several times in the early hours looking for me.

I was in the kitchen having breakfast; Mum and Dad were in the front room through the sliding glass doors. My dad had his glasses on and he was reading the paper, talking to Mum from behind it.

She said, 'We're going to have to do something about this.'

He agreed. 'Yeah, he's getting out of hand. Things are going too far, love.'

'What do you mean?' Anger in her voice.

'Michael,' he said.

'It's the police! They're picking on him and I'm getting absolutely sick of it!'

I watched the corner of the paper as it just . . . dropped. Dad looked her in the face, shook his head and said, 'It's absolutely pointless,' before carrying on reading. I was a hero in my mum's eyes. And the police were definitely the bad guys.

I felt happy. I loved my mother and our relationship grew very strong. She was like a lighthouse in a storm, always there for me. Wherever I went, whatever bad things I did, I could come home and feel safe.

My family was perfectly respectable, but I had taught myself to be bad. As I progressed through the ranks of criminal activity, my main buzz came from people not having a clue what I was doing. I had pockets of money and it made me laugh when they thought I was a builder or whatever. I felt I had control over others and that was really exciting.

I remember the first day I smoked a stone. The *power* I felt from it. It made me confident, aggressive even. People were making pipes out of cans and all sort of things, but I had my own little pipe. And I liked that – having the paraphernalia. It was nice. As I smoked that stone, I heard a tingling noise in my ears. My heart beat faster and faster, and there was a slightly anxious feeling in my stomach, but also a warmth. I felt as if I could jump ten feet high into the air. This was far better than snorting a line of cocaine – no comparison.

That began to be a bit of a problem. One hit is never enough for somebody like me, and stone is a very expensive habit. So I needed lots of money and that meant my illegal activity got worse and worse, and took me into a very dangerous world. At first, I stuck with little bits of stealing, little bits of fibbing. I'm not proud of it, but I have robbed everybody, from the young to the elderly, even my own children, even my father and mother.

But when you step into the real darkness, you lose the ability to pull the wool over people's eyes. You don't even try to lie about things – you just stop speaking about what you're doing altogether.

* * *

'Sit down, Michael. I've made you a nice cup of tea! With some biscuits – those chocolate ones you like . . . Now you know they're Michael's – don't touch them!'

Ahh, I love that woman!

'We're going to Manchester tonight.'

'*Where*, Mum?' I couldn't believe my ears. My mum and dad are going over to Manchester to walk round Piccadilly and give out cups of coffee, sandwiches and cigarettes to homeless people and prostitutes.

'What is wrong with you two?'

'What? No, it's God's work!'

I just shook my head. I was going over to Manchester that night as well. And they'd never know why. They'd gone to give; I was going to take.

I was beginning a new stage of life and so were they really. After Ann died, I'd watched them grieve together, heal together and become closer than they'd ever been. They'd go out and serve the poor and come back and tell these wonderful stories . . . I was a grown man, but I loved listening to my mother. She'd tell me about some lady who was a prostitute, shivering in the cold because she was wearing hardly anything at all, and I could picture it all in my mind and feel sorry for her – and I'd never even met her! Mum would say they'd given her a cigarette and a cup of coffee, and now they were going to start taking coats and blankets over whenever they visited. I thought they were nuts. Why would you go all the way over to Manchester just to help people?

Their faith in Jesus, especially my mother's, got very strong, and she had a born-again experience that changed her. She'd been praying for me for many years and, though she would never live to see the fruit of her prayers, she believed. She believed that I could change.

That first night they went over to Manchester, so did I – several hours later. I was picked up in a car and driven over. There was a job: we were to go to a house and take a large amount of money and drugs. The only thing was, it wasn't ours!

I remember sitting in the passenger seat listening to my friend, a big lad with many, many tattoos. The bravado! The rubbish coming out of his mouth! And as I heard the stories of the fights and the things he'd done, I thought, *Yes, you're tough. But you're not crazy enough. I am crazy enough!*

We got within a mile of the house and he stopped the car. Out we jumped. Then into the boot for the tools of the trade: a long-bladed implement that seems really dangerous but isn't too sharp; a bat that looks the part . . .

This is my first job, but I'm sure I'll be all right. And everything I get will belong to me! I'm still enjoying that thought when we get back in the car and my friend puts his hand under the seat. And pulls out something I'd never, ever seen close up in real life.

He passes it to me and I take it readily. No idea, *no idea* what to do with it, or how you'd even use it. But as I grasp it, I feel my hand grow warm . . . I feel power like I've never experienced before. It feels like an extension of me.

My head isn't thinking, I'm just *being*. I really like this thing. I put it to my nose and inhale it; I hold it against my face. I don't even know if it's loaded – if it has a safety catch. *I don't know!* But I act cool and put it in my pocket.

As we get close to the house, I'm thinking, *Right, I walk through the door and . . . My friend is far more experienced.*

1 Toddler Mick   2 First Communion
3 Family holiday (with sister Ann in red)   4 Aged 11

5 Teenage Mick 6 Family man, with eldest children
7 Mick, second wife and Jack 8 Mum and Dad

9–10 The Mad Mick Years 11–12 Marrying Sarah

13 Kathleen and Gordon, who took Mick in   14 With Dad and eldest sons
15 Graduation, with daughter Elle   16 Ordination, with Bishop Steven

17 Burnley cobbles 18–20 Delivering food parcels

21 Night mission   22 Prayer on the street
23 With Father Alex Frost

24 The Royal visit   25 The Duke and Duchess with Deacon and great-grandma

26 The Duchess and volunteers
27 The Duke greeting Sarah
28 Prayer with the Duke and Duchess

Very big, very strong, very tough. But not crazy. I decide then and there that this is the moment for Mad Mick to be born – and that's what I become. I've created my first persona.

Do we knock on the door? Do we try the door handle? Do we kick the door in? I decide to stand back, let him go through first. I'll just follow and see what happens.

There's a short path. It's dark, but there are lights on inside and one shines through the curtain, making a golden slot on the grass in front.

We go round the side. You can hear music, and when we get to the back door and find it wide open we can hear people inside too. My plan that he'll walk in first and I'll just follow goes completely out the window! Instead, I run in, shouting and screaming, creating as much noise as possible to intimidate. Straight into the front room, where there are two men and one woman, and immediately I've the back side of the blade (I'm not stupid) right against one of their throats.

I can't help myself. I put my hand in my pocket and pull out the . . . special thing. The *feeling* I get from it is like I've just shaken hands with the devil! So powerful. And as I point it directly across the room (my mind bizarrely taking in the orange seats on a brown settee and thinking, *Orange seats on a brown settee? How uncouth!*) the pretty young girl in the short skirt starts to scream and cry, but she soon stops when my friend shouts at her and pushes her. Things calm down a bit as I stay in the room and my friend ransacks the house. Then carrier bags full, stash in the boot, and we just drive away!

It felt as if everything had been in slow motion – as if my head had been under water, with all the noises subdued and on the outside. Had it even been real?

As we drove, we began to laugh. We pulled over in a dark layby and smoked a couple of stones each, and the adrenalin was good – really, really good. It was almost like that really pleasurable moment after sex, when you're just allowing yourself to feel . . . there's that sense of empowerment, before the feeling's lost. You see, crack allows you to feel that feeling. Unfortunately, as you keep smoking, though you try to get hold of that feeling again, you never quite manage to . . .

Back in town, I went to my friend's place and we carried the stuff into the house. I made a special effort to wipe down everything I'd touched – I wasn't too bothered about him! I even wiped the door handle in the car. There was nothing going to come back on me.

That special thing I had . . . I wiped it and felt a bit emotional having to give it back. It wasn't mine but I wanted to keep it.

My friend looked at me and said, 'You want one of them, don't you?'

'I do, yeah! Can you get me one?'

'I can.'

And that was another deal done. I'd be picking up my first 'thing' within a week.

Then to the spoils. Oh my God! Jewellery, *gold* jewellery – stupid amounts of it. Masses of weed. And yes, a lump of cocaine as big as my head. I'd never seen as much – there must have been half a kilo there. There was! Victory.

We started to count the money, over £5,000, and this was many years ago. It was a massive score. And so, so easy to do. Truly, money for nothing.

The only problem I could see was that (obviously) my friend knew me. He knew I'd been there. And as I started to think about that on my way home, I knew there were two choices: you either kill the people you work with after the job's done, or you work alone. And as the first option is probably going to get you a life sentence, it seems a good idea to go for the second.

You see, there's never any shortage of people wanting to turn other people over. Brothers and sisters, fathers and sons, husbands and wives – they've all snitched on their relatives to put me on to where money or drugs are. It's mind-blowing! You see, people are basically greedy and wicked, and they'll do anything for a touch – except the really bad stuff . . .

So from that day on, I decided to cut the odds. Mad Mick would always work out of town. And he'd only work alone.

The next day, I'm sitting talking to my mum and dad. They're telling me more stories and one's really special. They'd taken three flasks with them to Manchester, so they could give people cups of coffee. Two ran out eventually, as you'd expect, but the third never emptied all night. They were pouring and pouring and pouring, but the coffee just kept coming, and at the end they sat down and drank from it themselves!

Even then, the flask was full.

I laughed! I didn't believe a word of it! But many years later, when Dad mentioned this strange occurrence again, I did believe. You see, time and context can change everything.

* * *

I was never particularly afraid of the police. That was mostly due to arrogance – the feeling that I was always one step ahead, one step in front. But I hadn't thought things through.

You see, I was the kind of criminal who was a coward really. I wasn't likely to face you square on for a fight – more likely to punch you when you weren't looking! Slowly and surely over the next few years, I began to realize that I'd entered a world in which it's probably better to be caught by the police than by the people you've upset. I found out the hard way.

For now, though, I was on the gravy train. I had so many contacts around Manchester at this stage that work was coming in thick and fast. And I decided that the Mick who worked in that area wouldn't be the one I was at home.

So I got really shiny shoes, nice suits, ties, tie-pins, a fancy watch – all the things that people would take notice of. They wouldn't be looking at *me*, because they'd be looking at the things. The things weren't who I was, but it felt quite powerful when I met my new-found friends to be dressed differently, to speak slightly differently. And when I went home I'd be family man Mick – take the kids boxing and to the football, have tea with my wife. Nobody knew. That was the buzz. Nobody knew.

It was quite safe in Burnley. People assumed I was a businessman or a property developer, though in truth I was something else entirely. I never thought for one moment about the risk I was putting my family through – not only from the police but also from the criminal fraternity. It just never entered my head. You see, I've always been one of those people who does things without thinking about the consequences – until the consequences catch up with them. It's strange, but that's just who I am.

Within a really short time, it became obvious that picking up and dropping off merchandise was far more lucrative (not to mention less nasty) than burglary, so that's what I began to do. I'd travel to Manchester or Liverpool or Glasgow, sometimes to Leeds, and when I was away, I lived in a bizarre world; a world where ordinary rules simply didn't apply, because I was making them up myself.

Liverpool was jeans and T-shirts.

Glasgow was trackies, trainers and baseball caps.

Manchester was suits.

As I put different clothes on in different places, it felt as if I was putting on new skin; that I was becoming someone else.

During this time of my life, my drug use increased and I began to get more and more psychotic in my thinking – paranoid really. I would believe people were plotting against me when they weren't at all. The schizophrenic lifestyle was beginning to take its toll.

I remember being in Manchester one day when I realized I was wearing the wrong clothes. I had to leave, and it wasn't until I'd been home and changed that I could carry on with the job. You see, it was the persona who did the work – it wasn't really me. It's hardly surprising, given I was living with such a sense of dislocation, that I was having to be more and more creative just to survive my own mind.

There was one time I was in Glasgow. (A wonderful place – I really liked Glasgow. I could never quite make out what anyone was saying, but I loved the people. They were so straightforward. They were honest even in their dishonesty!) And I found myself in a pub. It's the kind of pub where you can smell yesterday's beer – stale – on the floor because it's not been mopped; it's got dark wooden tables, but when you look closely you can see fuzzy, ghostly images . . . the white frosting of ale and coffee and tea and whatever else has been on them. In short, it's the kind of pub where you wipe your feet on the way out rather than on the way in. But so full of characters . . .

There are four of us sitting round a table. They're talking (in Glaswegian) and I'm listening (because I need a guidebook); the ashtray's overflowing; the drinks are going down really, really well, and nobody cares whether you're using drugs or not. And as the conversation gets louder, well . . . you know how smoke rises? I've always thought sound does the same thing. You can sit still and hear it all above you, hanging in the air like smoke, just waiting to disperse.

In this rough pub with these tough people, I've one of those special things tucked down the back of my pants, a jacket over it, and a pocket full of something I shouldn't have had (a large pocketful, enough to get you six to ten years in jail!), when there's a sound, a distraction at the bar.

Two men have run in, and the guy leaning on the bar has been stabbed so many times, he's falling to the floor. And within minutes, you can see blue lights through the window, and everybody's scattering because they're carrying weapons or they're carrying drugs, or they just don't want to talk to the police.

There's no way out. The back exit is blocked, and the flashing lights are at the door.

I run behind the bar. There's a pinny up on a hook. In a second, I've got it wrapped around me and tied in really quite a nice neat bow at the front. The special thing and the pocket full of gear I drop straight into the ice bucket and cover over. The barman's just staring at me, but I put a finger to my lips, and as the police burst in and the ambulance comes and the questioning begins, I never have to answer a word! At an opportune moment, I leave with my pockets full again – and wet!

I walked away from all the chaos and noticed how beautiful the moon was that night. It looked so peaceful, it made me feel peaceful too – as if I'd won something and was just coming down.

I didn't really want to pull any drugs out and start smoking in the street, but I had a petrol lighter in my pocket so I had a little sniff of that, breathed it in nice and deep, just to change how I was feeling – that was always my way – and I got the usual comfortable little buzz. I remember thinking, *Life's pretty good. Life's pretty good.*

Next day I collected my money, and the conversation was all around where we had been hiding. One of my friends who'd slipped out the front door was behind a bush in the garden, one was up a tree somewhere, one was here, there and everywhere . . .

'And where were you? Where were you, Mick?'

'I was behind the bar. Wearing a pinny!'

The camaraderie – the laughter! You see, I could think on my feet, and when it came off, it was good. But when it didn't, I was afraid and (as I've said) I became dangerous.

The long drive home gave me the time to come back down to earth and I fell into contemplation. I started to think *Who the hell am I, really? I'm different people in different towns. I don't really know who I am.*

Another question sprang to mind: *Mick, what kind of things do you like?*

Well, apart from drugs and drink, I wasn't sure. I began to feel sad. I knew I was pretending to be different people; I knew that living my life this way wouldn't end well. The day would come when all these personalities would merge into one. Somebody would pull the plug.

And I would simply disappear down the drain.

8
'I WANT MY MU . . . DA . . . GRA . . .'

EVEN IN MY SAFE PLACE, my home, I was living a fantasy. I was proud of the house. It was mine. It was my kingdom. My wife was like my queen and the kids were princes and princesses.

I remember one summer morning, waking up early and sitting out on the patio, looking at the golden apples on the tree, and the beautiful pink and bright yellow roses we had. They were so alive and vibrant. A bee buzzed gently around, in for pollen and out . . . such peace.

And then, like thunder, a banging on the front door. I got up to unlock it and looked out – police! They're at the front, the back, the sides. There are cars and vans. And as I step hurriedly back inside, they're making to grab me as I duck and push and shout and try to have a conversation.

I end up just sitting there as they search the house for firearms – top to bottom. That's fine. I know there's nothing at home. I'm not that stupid.

My wife's distraught. My children are fascinated! Encouraged by me, they're also very cheeky towards the policemen. I got a great sense of pride from that. Sadly, I taught my children to hate authority. I was teaching them to be like me, which was strange really, when I didn't know who I was myself.

After hours of searching, being put in the back of a van and taken to the police station, I'm sitting in a cell, thinking about . . . nothing. Not afraid. Not excited. Not bothered. Just bored.

When they lead me to an interview room, I refuse to talk unless I can have a nice cup of coffee and a cigarette first. Of course, they want to talk. So I get my coffee and my cigarette. I've made my move in a game that continues with them asking, 'Do you want a solicitor?' before the interview kicks in. These are the days when interviews aren't videoed but they are voice recorded. So there's you, them, a table and a double-deck tape machine.

The questions begin.

'We found a firearm in your house. Can you tell us anything about that?'

What? They must have planted it; they must have put it there! There's no other explanation.

Yet these are two serious-looking detectives. They don't look like clowns. They look like intelligent human beings. And they have a case. One pulls a gun in a transparent evidence bag and says, 'For the benefit of the tape, I'm showing Mr Fleming a firearm found in his possession, underneath a tumble dryer in his kitchen.'

As I stared at it, I began to think, *Am I in a dream? Am I tripping off drugs? Am I in a TV show?* 'For the benefit of the tape, I'm showing Mr Fleming a firearm found in his kitchen.' I could feel the mirth rising up from my stomach. It just surged, it was completely uncontrollable. For four or five minutes I couldn't stop laughing. I ended up with my head on the desk and it was wet from my tears.

My response was really simple: 'For the benefit of the tape, you've got a banana with a strawberry stuck on the end of it, and you're showing me it's a plastic water pistol that's bright yellow with a red end. And I've got three children living in the house. For the benefit of the tape, are you mental?'

'There's no need for that kind of talk! We're asking you a serious question.'

'I've got nothing else to say. Charge me. Or release me. Charge me, please, for being in possession of a bright yellow water pistol with intent to wet people. Please.'

I was soon released with no charges, but I knew I was under investigation. Two days later, I was stopped for a road offence, yet after he had radioed through to get all my details, the police officer simply said, 'Right, on your way.' They weren't going to risk bringing me in for a stupid motoring offence after the water pistol incident. They were looking for something substantial.

I'd have to take care. Perhaps I'd stay home a bit more.

Sitting in my living room, I felt victory again. I felt untouchable. But they were searching.

Somebody must have been talking.

Somewhere.

* * *

The early hours of the morning, and a gigantic BANG on the front door. The noise erupted through the whole house.

I jumped up and pulled on a pair of tracksuit pants and stumbled around in the dark for the bat I kept beside the bed. I could hear my daughter screaming and the sound of feet running up the stairs. I thought, *This could be the day when I get seriously hurt.*

And then a loud cry: 'Armed police! Don't move!'

My little girl runs to me. She jumps and I catch her as the armed police rush into the room with torches and guns.

'Put the kid down! Put the kid down!'

'Not a chance. *Not a chance!* I'll go down fighting. You can kill me if you have to.' I felt this bravado inside me. You know the swirling sensation you get when you have a drink and it burns as it goes down and then hits your stomach and your eyes water slightly? I love that feeling! And I'm wanting something to happen. I'm wanting them to do something.

But it's not long before the adrenalin's fading. The hairs on the back of my neck, even on my hands, are standing on end.

'Put the child down, Mick.' Just to the side, there's a policewoman. 'Give me the little girl.'

Her long, tangled hair is in my eyes as she sobs, and I feel hatred towards the police. No notion whatsoever of anything I've done wrong – it's them! It's always been us and them.

In the end, I let them take the child. But instead of becoming submissive, I become aggressive and I find myself pinned down on the bed. Handcuffed. Thrown into the back of a van.

Here we go again.

The police had contacted Mum and I thank God for that woman. As my poor ex-wife was quite ill, Mum had become a mother to my children. I knew they'd be safe with her. But on the journey to the police station, I kind of wondered about why they'd come to the house with guns and all the screaming and shouting rather than arrest me someplace else. They knew there were youngsters there. I simply couldn't negotiate the thought of what might have happened to my children.

Of course, all the blame was on them.

Again there were questions. No answers. And I was released.

But the arrests were getting more and more frequent, and the truth was, my mental capacity was shot. I couldn't think properly. There were days when I couldn't breathe without a drink or a drug. And then I'd get that 'Thank God!' feeling – and I could start again.

I was driving my own car, not a stolen one, when I noticed a police car in the side-view mirror. It began to flash its lights and tried to pull me over. And I decided, in a split second, *I'm not going to stop! I'm sick of them harassing me. But I'm not going to break the law.*

So there I was in my bright red, shiny box, wondering how to tease and torment them. I rolled down the window and looked around for anything I could find to screw up and toss out – receipts, chewing-gum wrappers, anything! They'd be observing and wondering if I was offloading drugs perhaps – surely someone would need to go back to check? And that would cost them precious time.

But driving down the road – at thirty miles an hour, not speeding – I began to realize that there wasn't only one car now: there was a convoy of police vehicles and vans, and among them was a 4x4 I recognized as the armed response vehicle. I had no weapons on me, no drugs, just quite a lot of money in my pocket, but that's not a crime.

I turned left down a hill and noticed a school playing field. Children were running around and teachers supervising – the perfect place to stop, because the police wouldn't do anything there. I pulled over. There was a police car in front, one behind and one at the side. Nowhere to run. Nowhere to hide. I sat still.

Loud shouts: 'Get out the vehicle! Get out the car! GET OUT OF THE CAR!'

I turned to see many, many officers surrounding my shiny red box. They were pointing firearms right at me! I smiled, kissed the window and lit up a cigarette. I felt like a live fish in a tin can. I could see all these eyes glaring at me, and to me it seemed as if they were afraid. But I wasn't.

As I took another drag of the cigarette, I looked at my own eyes in the mirror. The person reflected wasn't me again – I didn't know which Mick it was this time. Everything was becoming scrambled. I remember seeing a curling eyebrow and a kind of discolouring to my face, a greyish tinge . . . the colour people are just before they die. But the smile! How can you smile when you're surrounded by armed police screaming and shouting at you?

As I blew the smoke and it hovered around the car, I thought, *What to do now?* All I had left was rebellion. Within a moment, I heard the smash of the back window, so when an officer with a stick raised it to smash the one at the front, I put my face right against it.

Ah, so they're not really that keen on hurting me at this stage. Maybe they think I've got a gun. Maybe they think I'm just crazy. That made me smile even more. Something in me felt pretty evil – and I liked it.

Then CS gas filled the car. The smell, the taste! I could see the bloodshot veins in the whites of my eyes – they were burning, running. I was going to have to get out of the vehicle.

As I opened the door, coughing and streaming, it was like looking through frosted glass. I could only make out vague shapes, and there were so many voices in the chaos.

An officer approached: 'Lie on the ground! Lie on the ground face down! Put your hands behind your back! Lie down!'

To be compliant would have seemed sensible to most people – if you didn't want to die.

But I didn't want to live! So with a huge push, I grabbed one of the officers around the neck and threw him over the bonnet of the car. We wrestled and rolled until I was gassed once again. Dragged off the officer. Held down on the pavement and cuffed.

I stopped squirming and fighting because I knew it would do no good – maybe I was crazy, maybe I wasn't. The taste of tarmac in my mouth – it wasn't nice. They poured water into my eyes and gave me a drink. And as they were searching the vehicle, I was thrown into a van. Then we were off.

They paraffin-tested the vehicle for traces of firearms and whatever else. I wasn't charged, but I knew things were closing in. Many years later, when I read the depositions for the case, I was horrified: 'We spotted Fleming's vehicle at three o'clock. We radioed through for permission to draw firearms on the vehicle and shoot if necessary. Ten past three: We stopped Fleming and drew firearms.'

I was so close to being shot, so close. I wanted to die. But I didn't really have the bottle to kill myself, so I thought I could be like Butch Cassidy and the Sundance Kid and go out in a blaze of glory. I'd run out and they'd pull me down and I'd be this hero, this folk hero who would live on for ever.

The real world isn't like that, though. In the real world, children sob for their mums and dads. The night of the incident, free again, I lay in my bed alone, and in the next

room my beautiful little girl: 'I want my mu . . . da . . . gra . . .'
Those cries have haunted me for many years. A little girl who
didn't know who to cry for when she was in distress.

You see, crime and drugs do that to families – they tear
them apart inside, so slowly. I was lucky to have a good
father and a good mother. They'd become parental role
models for my children. And very selfishly I let them.

9
JESUS IN A SHOP DOORWAY

I WAS APPROACHING THE FINAL FALL. The biggest fear of my life was about to become a reality. All bets were off after that.

It seemed a normal morning. A drink. A drug. A shave. Dress smartly. *I know where I'm going today*, I thought, little realizing there was only two hours to go before the thunderstorm, the hurricane, the tsunami . . .

'Michael, it's your dad! Can you come as quick as possible? Your mum's collapsed!'

I flew round. I was always good at keeping my head in an emergency, but as I ran into the house, I could see my dad was in pieces. He told me Mum was upstairs in the bathroom. She'd had a stroke and was lying on the floor, unresponsive. I got him to ring for an ambulance, and as we waited I sat beside her thinking how beautiful she still looked with her hair dyed, dark and wavy. I noticed she had little red lines on her cheek, broken veins . . .

'Mum,' I said, 'if you can hear me, just squeeze my hand.' A slight pressure! I got to say something that I don't think I'd ever said and meant to anyone: 'I love you, Mum. I love you.'

The panicked voice of my dad on the phone, and then him calling my sisters . . . I felt calm. I was in the middle of chaos and I already knew Mum wouldn't pull through. But it was all right, because I was in the moment.

The ambulance came and rushed us to hospital and we took her in . . . and I left. You know in the movies when there's been a big explosion and the villain, or even the hero sometimes, turns his back as everything's falling apart around him and just walks off? That was me. I left my dad and my sisters to it. My bit was done and I needed a drink. I really needed a drink.

There was vodka in the side pocket of the car. As I undid the lid, it smelt stronger than normal. The bottle itself looked brighter, the label was shiny and the contents were dancing inside. I took my first swig. Felt the burn. And then smashed it. Aah . . . so much better. As I fastened the lid, I noticed the scar on the palm of my hand.

What I wouldn't have given to turn the clock back.

* * *

Another phone call on another day: 'You need to come to the hospital, Michael. We have to say our final goodbyes.'

As I walked in, I didn't feel anything. I already knew she wasn't coming home. I just knew.

My sister and my dad were in tears in the tiny family room at the side. They let me go through on my own, and I took her by the hand and said, 'Can you hear me, Mum?' This time there was no answering squeeze. I don't think she knew I was there. Her breathing was horrendous; it made me think of a tractor – so heavy and echoey – and I realized it was a death rattle. She was getting closer and closer to the end. I thought, *I hope she's not in pain – because I am.*

As I looked down, I noticed her handbag. I don't know why it was even there. What possible use could she have for it now? I put my hand in. Opened her purse. And saw a twenty pound note. 'I'll be having that, Mum. You're not going to have any need for it.' I knew where my mind was going.

I walked out of the room without looking back. I didn't kiss her on the forehead – that only happened in my dreams later. I didn't stroke her face and say, 'Mum, I'm going to miss you and I really love you.' I so wish I had. I just told my family, 'I'm not hanging around.' And I left.

I walked into a pub nearby, pulled out the twenty pound note and stared at the Queen's face on it. That curly hair . . . my mum did look a bit like the Queen!

'Treble vodka, no ice . . . No, I don't want coke. Just treble vodka and keep them coming.'

Three glasses later, I'm calm and relaxed.

And then the phone call: 'She's gone . . . she's gone.'

Time to go and score. Got my drugs and spent two hours avoiding all feelings whatsoever. Then a final drink. A trusty bottle of vodka. A bottle that never lets you down. It felt quite cold in my hand as I pulled it out of the side pocket, but I knew it would make me feel warm inside. And as I took a swig, another laugh arose from the pit of my stomach. You see, laughing's a good way of avoiding real emotions. But the laughs that came out of me then were more like cackles, vile sounds that were out of context – almost like a loud scream in the middle of a love story that shouldn't be there.

I felt evil had taken a real grip on me.

And it had.

* * *

Sometime before this, I had married again. But there was a cunning plan attached to that! We would live in separate

105

houses so I could carry on doing what I was doing and she would never know. My wife was a lovely woman and I had another child with her. Now there were four in all.

However, with the death of my mother, my addictions just seemed to spiral out of control, and my ability to think and to act were diminished greatly. I didn't know who or what I was any more. And the result was that I just walked away.

From everything. And everyone.

I found myself in strange towns, sitting on benches. Lost. Though I had a flat to stay in, I would sleep on the street, as it felt more comfortable. After six or seven days of this, I stumbled into a church. I was very ill, very dishevelled, but there were nice people in this warm building. It had tables with plastic covers on so you didn't mark them and very comfortable chairs. They gave me toast – golden and heavily buttered (it smelt like the toast my mum had made for me when I was a boy) – with a nice cup of tea. Sweet tea and toast, so comforting.

It was getting late and I could see these good Christian people were wondering how they could get rid of me. They were trying to be kind, yet looking at the clock. It was cold outside, *so cold*. I only had a T-shirt. A man and a lady were talking and gesturing and looking over. They were going to ask me to leave! And I didn't know where to go.

'I have to lock up now, Michael, but please feel free to come again next week, and I hope everything works out okay for you.'

As I left the church, the chill I felt wasn't from the wind or the breeze; it was from the people inside. Nice people, but they knew nothing. I wasn't part of their gang and they wouldn't let me in.

Where was your God?

Stumbling down the road I saw a guy with a quilt wrapped around him. He waved me over: 'What you doing?'

'I really don't know,' I said.

'Where you sleeping?'

'Anywhere I can.' My legendary arrogance was scarcely in evidence any more.

'Sit down.' He almost commanded it.

I had nothing left inside me to argue, so I did as he said and he shared the quilt with me. He had a dark woollen hat on his head. I remember the smell as he took it off – a bit whiffy yet comforting. He put the hat on my head and I felt instantly warmed. Then he reached to his side, opened his bottle of cider and began to pour it into my mouth. Slow sips. The shakes started to ease off, and slowly but surely calmness returned. In ten minutes, he'd fed me my medicine and I felt well. He put a cigarette in my mouth and lit it for me.

I met Jesus that day. Jesus cared for the sick. He loved the poor. He lived with the poor. I couldn't find him in the church, but I found him in a shop doorway.

Where else would he have been?

* * *

Living rough when there was no need . . . Maybe I was punishing myself. I could smell my own body odour and I always had a knife with me. I kind of hoped someone would try and attack me or mug me or something . . . anything. You see, my mind was whirling and whirling so fast and I just wanted it to stop. I was back to thinking I just wanted to die. And I was killing myself, but very slowly.

One day I was sitting on the ground near some bins at the back of a supermarket, and a young couple came by – a pleasantly spoken middle-class boy with his hippy girlfriend; you know, the type who always want to help. It's so easy, *so easy*, to manipulate nice people like that. You can take what you want from them. And then, when you've got them in the palm of your hand, you can just squeeze tighter – till you crush them.

I remember noticing that she had lots of different-coloured beads in her hair and a very nice smile. Slightly plump, but very pretty. And he was just . . . well, a college kid – the kind whose hair was slightly too long, who wanted to have an earring but daren't because what would Mummy say?

They approached me and asked if I needed anything. Did I want a sandwich?

Oh dear. I've got to the stage where people are wanting to buy me sandwiches. My life's not going too well really! But they were nice people. I said I wouldn't mind a cigarette.

'We don't smoke.'

'Oh. Okay.'

'Can we ask you some questions?'

'No. Because you don't smoke.'

Within two minutes they were back with a packet of cigarettes. I put one in my mouth and lit it. It was comforting. It almost felt like breastfeeding: the reassurance a baby gets from the warmth of his mother. I tasted the smoke and blew it out.

Turned out they were both students and they were learning about addiction and homelessness. And with me they'd found a real test case. He had a pad and pen.

'There are just two questions we'd like to ask you. What does it feel like to live the kind of life that you live? And what do you think the future holds?'

I sat there gazing up at the sky on that cold, grey day and as I exhaled, the cigarette smoke mingled with the air until I could no longer distinguish between the two. The couple were uncomfortably crouched beside me. I could see the slight pain on their faces and I wondered why they didn't sit down. Would it have made them too much like me? I knew they wanted to be polite. They waited and eventually I said, 'Give me the pen and paper.'

What does it feel like to live the kind of life that you live? And what do you think the future holds? I looked at a blank page and imagined how I could rewrite my life from the beginning, and I began to feel a little smile coming. But no, that wasn't real. What did happen, miraculously, as I put pen to paper, was that the words flowed. I've thought about it many times over the years, and I know I had no ability to produce what I did. I couldn't even write in a straight line. (At that time I couldn't walk in one either.)

The cold winds wrap around his body, like a spiteful lover
The dark echo of his breath slowly disappearing into a distant silence. The familiar smell of an old friend who would never desert him lay heavy on his breath. Home on the street, but no door and never a key. Once a father, never a son. Flashes of a man that never was. A victim from the age of eleven. A child that forgot how to cry. Nightmares that unpacked but would never leave. To sleep, to smile, to feel the touch of humanity, were all things for others. Finding a god in a needle and love in a pipe.

How much longer?
He asks for nothing and he receives it in abundance.
Flashing lights. A strange unfamiliar warmth. Distant
voices. A brilliant blinding blackness. No one to cry.
No one to leave flowers. A nameless face, neither
forgotten nor remembered.
Then the wind blew again, and they all turned away.

I remember looking at their faces as I handed them the
paper. They stood up (I'm sure I heard one of their knees
crack) and huddled together to read the scribbles. I could see
a black tear running down the girl's face through the layers
of mascara; just trickling, until it dropped to the ground. He
put his arms around her and they wept.

A description of hopelessness.

And it was me.

Years later I met the guy again – he's a worker in drug and
alcohol services – and he remembered me. He'd kept what
I'd written! He had it on his phone and he told me how it had
inspired him. I too have kept those words close to my heart.

I felt sure that day that I would die on the streets.

But I was wrong.

* * *

I'd begun to hate my father because my mother had died. I
needed somebody to blame and he was sort of an easy target.
I never wanted to do him any violence; I just didn't want to
like him.

I turned up at his house because I wanted something of
my mother's – a reminder, a keepsake, I said, but I think
I really wanted some jewellery so I could sell it and buy

drugs. All he handed me was a Bible. A *Bible*! It had been my mum's. It seemed almost like an insult. I looked at it, then back to his face, and I could see a look in his eye I hadn't been aware of before. He wasn't afraid of me, but he had become wary, very wary. I knew my own father could see the potential I had for evil. As I left the house with the Bible, I heard the click of the key turning in the lock. It felt as if the door had definitely been closed, and something in me died, once again.

I had taken the Bible because I didn't want my father to have it, not because I wanted it. It would be years before I'd even look inside it. But when I did, what *joys* I found! Mum had been praying for me for years and years. And there were letters from friends from all over the country who had been praying for me too.

I can tell you today that the prayers of a loving mother, from the heart, are always answered.

* * *

My different personas and personalities were becoming hopelessly muddled. Even people who didn't know me were starting to take notice. I'd be in pubs with long knives sticking out the top of my jacket. I'd carry tasers and special things in my pocket, because the weaker and more unstable I became, the more my fear increased. I was in the situation of trying to protect myself – from me! And that's always a dangerous place to be. Like a building where the demolition machines had moved in, I was being knocked down, a wall at a time. I'd begun doing things in my home town that I would only ever have done in other places before. All my careful planning went out the window. There were no drawings and working-outs. There was just a sickness.

On one of those sick days, I was in a pub drinking.

'Triple vodka over here, love!' And another. And another. 'No ice, just vodka.'

At the bar to my right, I noticed a very fleshy-looking geezer. Beautiful suit and what a lovely watch – it sparkled on the bar and I knew what make it was. He had money. His suit really fitted (any time I buy a suit, it never looks like that!) and he was just perfect in it. One of those blokes, with the suit and the thousands of pounds' worth of watch . . . And as he bought his drinks, he didn't pull out a wallet, he pulled out a wad of money. As I clocked it, I decided that was my money – he was spending my money. He was spending my fucking money! You see, my mind suggested things like that and told me they were real. So I was going to take my money back.

He walked into the toilets and I followed. I pulled out the special thing from my pocket and put it right against his face, pushed him against the wall and put my arm across his throat. The tan-looking colour drained out of him, and his skin and slick hairdo just seemed to melt into one. He was petrified. He willingly offered me everything he had. I thought for a moment about taking the watch, but I didn't need a watch and I didn't really want one. So I just pocketed the money and left. A good score, but mugging people in toilets? Me? The criminal expert? The mastermind? More like a thug. A disgrace.

I thought I'd better get rid of the special thing right away, so I did. I went and put it where it needed to be. And then into another pub for another drink, chatting to a young lady I really liked, though she always wore funny shoes: high heels that were very feminine, but never the right colour! She would have a black dress on and bright red shoes. It never seemed quite correct to me. But she was very pretty and I remember buying her drinks just to get some sort of response from her – just to see if I could feel something. It was like playing a game.

I remember she put her drink down and there was lipstick on the rim. It looked fake – an empty naked glass with those lips on the outside. And that's what I was like: naked and empty, just searching for a feeling. Needing to be loved and touched.

I went outside to the front of the pub – it was my local, everybody knew me, it was a safe place for me – and lit a cigarette. And as I looked across the road, I could see policemen crouching down behind a car. I could see the uniforms, I could see their heads!

I thought, *Something's happening. Something's going down.* I went back inside. I had some drugs on me – not a lot, but enough to get me in trouble. So I passed them to a friend, who gladly received them, shook my hand and put them away. I'd never see them again. It was a good transaction.

Back outside. Waiting, waiting for them to pounce. What would happen now?

There was movement to the right, to the left, and I walked out of the carpark on to the road, slowly, taking everything in. I could pick out every motor, every hidden policeman. This looked like a big operation.

And then officers with firearms and that familiar chant: 'Lie on the floor! Get down on the floor! Armed police!'

Again! I just loved it. I thought, *What happens if I run? Do they shoot me? Let's see!* I set off at pace, running as fast as I could, across the road, down the back street, police in pursuit, cars following. Eventually, broken and tired, lost and drunk, they caught up with me. And then a huge scuffle and me punching a policeman and rolling about in the dirt and the filth and the mud . . .

Looking up and seeing the streetlight shining down on us, I began to laugh. It seemed so funny that I'm fighting the police and there's guns and cars and I'm in that familiar movie once again.

Arrested. But there's nothing to find. The tools had gone back in the toolbox. There was just me and the money. It's not an offence to have money, and very difficult to prove if it's someone else's or not.

You'd never think that people who were criminals with nice suits and watches would ring the police. But you see not everybody follows the rules. As I was cuffed and taken away, I knew I had to follow my rules. Nothing to say. Nothing to say. Released. But so poorly, so lost. I didn't know who I was; I didn't know what I wanted. Anybody could have taken me anywhere.

I was like a dog wearing a lead. Just wandering and hoping somebody would pick up the lead. And pat me, feed me, take me in.

But they never did.

Until, like all strays, I ended up in the pound.

The psychiatric unit.

10
McDONALD'S SHOWDOWN

IN THE EARLY YEARS of my sobriety, I knew I was still ill, but I was getting better. I'd had the meltdown and been poured into this new mould. I'd listened to the angel and spent time rebuilding my relationships. So when people asked me, 'How're you doing, mate?' I'd always say, 'I'm doing really well. I'm clean, I'm sober, I haven't used in . . . Yeah, I'm praying as well, you know. Man, I feel good.'

Well, the truth was, I didn't. I still had all this stuff inside me. I didn't want it to be there but it was, and I didn't know what to do. How would I change? I was definitely better than I'd been. I was definitely better sober. But how do you stay sober? How do you stop yourself going back?

Helping other people seemed to motivate me and contribute to my recovery. I was drawing strength from my own weakness. And I would always pray.

Having inhabited so many different personalities over the years, a part of me still hankered to be someone else. But I was pretty sure there were no more reinventions left in me, no more personas. I was just going to have to find out who I really was and try to live the best I could.

I'd built a wonderful relationship back with my dad. After all the horrendous stuff I'd done – selling his house from underneath him; spending his money; spitting in his face when he was in a hospital bed and wishing him dead – I really began to love him. I would end up nursing him and driving him around – we really got to know each other before he finally passed away. It made me proud that I'd learned to stop hating the right people.

But in my dreams still . . . that dark aroma of sweat and sweetness, those tinges of alcohol. I'd find myself waking up choking. He wouldn't seem to go, you see. I only needed to smell something, see something, hear a piece of music, and I'd be back there. I wasn't quite as afraid. I wasn't carrying any weapons. I'd been hammering the gym so hard, I looked really strong and fit, but I still didn't truly know who I was.

I would sit in cafés, drinking coffee and watching the world go by; looking at couples as they strolled down the street holding hands, and wondering why I'd never been affectionate like that. I watched a father walk by with his child – he ruffled his hair; he had a big smile on his face; he was proud. And the little lad laughed. I never had anything like that.

I'd hear people ordering food and then become frustrated because the food didn't come quickly enough. I began to notice myself noticing things, and that was good. It felt as if I was being reprogrammed.

I started to wonder if I needed some counselling to help me come to terms with all the people I'd hurt. And with all the people who had hurt me. Seeing as I'd turned into one of those strange praying people, I thought I'd better ask God if he would help me out. But I made a funny decision that surprised even me. I always said 'in the name of Jesus' at the end of each prayer, but I'd heard a little whisper that all the power came from the Holy Ghost. So I decided to ask him.

My prayer was simple: 'Holy Ghost, set me free from all this horrible stuff I feel inside. I'm struggling a bit, mate, and I don't know what to do. So I'm chucking this one to you, and I'm just going to leave it with you. And if I need to do anything, give us a shout! In Jesus' name. Amen . . . And also, thank you, Father', because I thought I'd better hedge my bets. If there's three of them, I'd better speak to them all!

I later found out that all three were the same, all at once, all at the same time, and that didn't half mess with my head. But hey, we've all got to learn.

Within forty-eight hours, I had an experience that I hold in my heart and mind to this day, such was the enormity of its impact. It transformed my life. But be warned, the story I'm about to tell is not for the faint-hearted.

Just a normal day. Chilly outside, with a little bit of rain in the air and leaves swirling down the road in the wind. Another day sober and that should have been enough, though to be honest it wasn't, because I felt I wasn't truly living. I really wanted more.

I began talking to my new pal the Holy Ghost, and Jesus and the Father. I wasn't getting much back. To be honest, it felt like a one-way street!

I went into McDonald's and bought a coffee. I took the lid off because I always like to see what I'm drinking, and I like to breathe in as I sip, so I'm tasting and smelling the coffee at the same time – it's as if your senses become more alert. As I put the cup down, I looked across the restaurant and directly opposite I saw a man sitting alone. You could tell he'd had a drink. There were strange sounds coming out of his mouth that weren't coherent, and he was banging his head backwards against the wall. Mothers with children nearby were deliberately moving away, and I heard someone say something to one of the workers behind the counter. But it seemed she didn't have the heart to ask him to leave.

I stood up and got closer. Something strangely familiar about his face . . . he'd lots of lines and looked as if he hadn't shaved for about three months. A grey beard, and a nose that was just a little bit bent out of shape . . . just a little bit. He had that alcoholic smell about him, that blend of sweat and sweetness . . . I looked at his hands and they were trembling. I sat down next to him and asked if he wanted a coffee or something to eat.

He lifted his face and I saw his eyes, familiar eyes, eyes that I seemed to know. Dark and lost. 'Yeah. I'll have a burger.'

I got him a burger and a coffee, and sat and listened as he told me many things about his life. He spoke about his family and his children. He told me his name and I told him mine.

He smiled and he laughed. But I didn't.

I gave him a small amount of money for the bus. And my phone number. Arranged to meet him again.

I knew him.

And I hadn't killed him.

There was always another day.

* * *

I didn't sleep that night. I tossed and turned, my mind like a washing machine, whirling and spinning. The pain and scars and wounds of the past were tearing me inside. I noticed the light was shining through the curtain, but this time there were no faces. There was nothing.

I went downstairs in the early hours of the morning to make myself a coffee, and lit a cigarette. Waiting for the kettle to boil I opened the drawer, and as I was reaching for a spoon I saw the long knives with their razor-sharp edges. I pulled one out and its cold black handle fitted perfectly into the palm of my hand, like it belonged there. I remember holding the sharp end against the side of my face, just to feel it, and running my fingers along the blade . . .

It spoke to me.

I left it out, waiting for the morning.

Lying in bed again, I wasn't afraid; just in turmoil. But I didn't cry. I didn't bite my pillow!

When I awoke and looked out the window, I saw there was nothing special about the day. It wasn't dark but it wasn't bright. The feeling in the pit of my stomach was very hard to define.

As I put my coat on and picked up my wallet and my keys, I stared down at the knife with the black handle. I knew I'd have to take it with me. I might never get this opportunity again. I put it in my inside pocket and glanced in the mirror on the way out the door. The old me just wasn't there. There was no adrenalin. There was very little emotion. But still, I had to do what I had to do.

I pulled into the carpark ten minutes early – a bit of thinking time, a bit of cigarette time. The memories just came flooding back. I could smell the smells, I could hear the threat: 'You speak a word of this, I'll kill your parents! Do you understand?' I put my hand to my throat and pulled the invisible hand away. This time! This time I'd pick up the bottle and smash him round the face with it. This time I wouldn't be a victim.

As I walked into the restaurant, I pulled the knife from my inside pocket and slipped it up my sleeve. Handle first.

He was there. In the exact same seat. He smiled, and as I walked over he stood up and held out his hand to be shaken.

And then it happened. My mind took over. My mind pushed him against the wall, flicked my arm, caught the handle of the knife, pushed it into the side of his neck and twisted it, swearing, cursing, spitting at him as he fell to the seat and blood poured out. I kneed him in the face. I jumped on him! People screamed and cried. I pulled the knife out again and slashed him. I cut him. I took a piece of his ear off and held it in my left hand, squeezed it like I squeezed that fifty pence piece! Then I turned away and walked out the door.

But that was just in my mind.

You see, I wasn't afraid. I wasn't that scared little boy. I'd become a man.

How do you exchange greetings with the wrong hand? That's what I did. I shook his hand and I sat down next to him. And *he* went and bought the coffees. He was more sober than the day before. His eyes were different to how I remembered them – they had colour in them; they were brown not black.

He told me about his alcoholism and again I found myself saying very little. As I looked him up and down – his tattered, smelly clothes and matted hair – I couldn't believe I'd been afraid of this man all my life. I almost pitied him.

When would I tell him? How would I tell him?

I felt the knife still up my sleeve and was worried it might fall out, so I went to the toilet and concealed it in my pocket.

I washed my hands, and as I raised my head I saw my reflection in the mirror.

There was no darkness in my eyes.

I couldn't understand why I didn't hate. Why I couldn't do it. Then I remembered my prayer to the Holy Spirit, and the feeling I'd had in my stomach. It wasn't hatred.

I'd been changed.

When I joined him again, the conversation was around AA and recovery. At this point I knew I had a number of choices: I could tell him; I could go to the police; I could walk away and never see him again; I could have him killed. Or I could help him.

I decided to help him get sober. And that's what I did. Over the next few months, he began to recover. However, the damage he'd done through alcohol over the years took a heavy toll and within two years he was dead.

But he died sober.

And he died not knowing that I knew he was the man who raped me.

* * *

From that point on, it was as if I was no longer trapped, as if the chains had been broken and just fallen off. I didn't dream. There were no nightmares, there were no fears, there were no anxieties. I remember walking down the street and thinking it was as if my legs didn't belong to me because they were without stiffness! I had no pain in the back of my neck where I'd been stressed and tight for years.

I began to feel the love of God.

You see, forgiveness isn't saying everything's all right. Forgiveness is saying I'm no longer going to live in your sin.

I'm no longer going to let what you did control me. My sin has been hard enough to come to terms with – I'm definitely not going to live in yours.

I stopped being a victim. I stopped talking like a victim, thinking like a victim and living in this pit I could never quite climb out of. That Holy Spirit geezer knew a thing or two. I asked him, and he put the very man I needed to see right in front of me again after thirty-odd years! And I had a choice, because forgiveness is a choice. Yet I'd felt guided; I didn't feel as if I'd forgiven him in my own strength.

Offering that forgiveness has changed *everything* in my life. It's changed how I look at things. It's changed how I see. It's changed how I feel. It's shown me how to let go. Most of all, it's taught me the love of God.

God forgives. And I was forgiven. The other man? I leave that between him and God. It's none of my business any more. Freedom comes from the love of God. And he'd poured his grace into me. And I was able to do what was impossible.

I was able to let go.

11
POSH CAKES AND DELIVERANCE

IF YOU'RE USED TO LIVING with pain and victimhood, living without them isn't actually all that easy! But then I thought nothing in my life had ever been easy. And things could only be better than they were.

I smile as I remember now, but I began to get a kind of craving to find out more about God, having seen this Holy Spirit geezer doing these crazy things. I imagined him flying all over the world, just zapping people's heads and stuff, changing situations and circumstances, and then having a laugh with Jesus: 'Never guess what I've done! Know that fella, that Mick, yeah? Ha ha ha, he's only gone and . . .' And the Father looking at me and feeling sort of proud. And they're all one! Maybe I was growing into a theological understanding of God. If so, it was developing through my own experience and what I was seeing around me.

I wondered about pain. I wondered about Jesus on the cross and the way he suffered. And I started to be really grateful, even for all the bad things I'd done. Instead of feeling guilty about them, I realized my new friend the Holy Spirit was convicting me. He was telling me they were wrong. My prayers began to change. I thanked God that Jesus loved me so much that he was releasing me from my sin; that through his death I was able to see what I truly was. And although that was painful, I had great joy.

You see, the cross turned things inside out, upside down and back to front. My story was the Jesus story. My story was that of every Christian: if only we'll go through the pain, our lives – and those of others around us – will be transformed.

By this time my dad was in his eighties, in his twilight years, and we'd go out together and talk and laugh. I'd take one of my sons with me and he got to know his grandad so well. We became a regular sight every weekend in the local coffee shops, sipping our lattes and talking about football and life and things, and God. So many stories – too many to tell . . .

One day I was with Dad in his little one-bedroom bungalow. It was quite trendy, you know! My sisters had picked the fancy blue wallpaper, and he had all mod cons. His sight was very poor – he'd lost an eye in the Second World War when he was seventeen, though he never really liked to talk about that, and his good eye had begun to deteriorate.

Sitting on his favourite comfy chair, with his hands spread out on the arms, he said to me, 'Mick, will you pray for me knee?' He had bad joints, you see, and he'd started to walk with a stick, which he hated because he was such an independent man. He loathed the idea of becoming frail.

'So will you ask God to fix me knee?'

Hmm . . . this is my dad, and I'd have to pray out loud in front of him and say words and stuff.

'Yeah, course I will, Dad,' came out my mouth. But inside I felt awkward, so I thought I'd better ask my new mate, this Holy Spirit geezer, because he seems to know what he's doing, you know? I think he'll have a laugh at this one!

I put my hand on my dad's knee and began, 'Holy Spirit . . .' I'm just about to say, 'If it's all right with you, my dad's knee's a bit sore. Can you just fix it and make it all right again? In Jesus' name. Amen.'

But what came out my mouth was nothing like that at all. It went something like this: 'Lord, this is my dad who I love dearly. Lift away from him the memories and the thoughts and the pain of catching his daughter in his arms and lowering her lifeless body to the floor. And heal his knee. Take away the emotional and physical pain, if it's your will. Amen.'

A deadly silence. It seemed as if even the clock had stopped ticking. As if the telly wasn't on. There was no sound and a stillness in us both. We were like mannequins. It felt as if an hour had passed, but it was only minutes.

And then Dad stood up, tears in his eyes. And he walked across the room, painless. 'He's only bloody fixed it, Mick! He's only bloody fixed it! Look, check this out!' He's bending his knee. He's dancing. He's trying to do an Irish jig! And there was such a huge smile on his face – one of those smiles that's so infectious you simply have to smile yourself.

I felt powerful, but yet with no power. It was such a strange feeling. God had used me. Even me, this crackpot! My dad's leg was definitely all right. I wondered, *Where do we go from here?*

I was beginning to grasp a little bit of theology, but I thought I'd better start listening to more YouTube stuff about Jesus. So I hit the Sermon on the Mount, because it was Jesus talking, and I thought, *That's where you want to be, lad. You definitely want to be at the opposite end of Jesus talking! Get that in your ears, and let's see what happens.*

It was brilliant, amazing stuff. It really excited me. I wasn't terribly keen on the bit that said to gouge your eyes out and chop your arms off and stuff, because that came too close to things I'd actually seen. So I kind of dismissed that section because I didn't understand it.

And the Bible was rather like that for me. Most of it I didn't understand.

* * *

One day my dad and I drove over to my sister's house in the next town. She was a school teacher – sensible, middle class, a beautiful lady. And we sat out in her garden. Very posh. Lovely shrubs! Nice cup of tea (out of a teapot, of course) and cakes. Not like the cheap cakes I'd buy. Oh no, no, no! These were handmade cakes with cream and, to be fair, they do taste better!

As we sat in the garden munching the high-quality cakes, the conversation turned to God. Dad began to tell my sister about his leg and all about Jesus. She became . . . interested. But there was a look on her face I'd seen on myself. It was almost distorted. I had an urge to pray, but I didn't; I pushed it back down inside. I knew if we prayed for her, something was going to happen. In any case, thinking about my past life, it felt crazy that I was even contemplating such a thing.

But then these words came out of her mouth: 'I feel so unwell – I've felt like this for a long time. Will you pray for me?'

And I said, 'Yeah!'

I got the same little feeling as before, that this is going to get embarrassing. We're outside, there may be neighbours in the garden next door because the sun's shining; I've got my dad here, and you want me to pray with you over a cup of tea and a nice cake!

'I'll give it a shot.'

I had to go to my old pal again. I always have to do that; I always have to dig in. Someone told me that the Holy Spirit geezer lives in me. So it's quite easy really. I don't have to make a telephone call or shout loudly, because I'm taking him around everywhere I go. I can ask him anything!

So I did. I said, 'Holy Spirit, me old pal, this is our kid, our Sarah, and she's not right. She doesn't feel right; she feels something's wrong – physically, spiritually, emotionally. Can you help her? In Jesus' name—'

I hadn't even finished speaking when she began to cry. Her long dark hair was in her eyes as the tears started to run, but they were almost tears of anger. I saw her fists clenching, her body so uncomfortable, twisting this way and that in the metal outdoor garden chair. As I looked her full in the face, I saw her eyes were large and black – her irises didn't exist any more, the pupils had taken over – and I simply said, 'In Jesus' name, leave her be.'

I've never seen anything like it. She ended up on the floor on her hands and knees, howling like a dog, howling like a wolf. She began to shout and curse. My father was in shock, but I said, 'Don't worry, Dad. Just keep praying; keep praying to Jesus. Just keep asking Jesus to look after her.'

So he kept praying and I kept praying . . . and then, just in an instant, it was as if a switch was turned on and a light appeared in her eyes. She sat down, drained and sodden with tears and saliva. We'd seen a miracle. My sister accepted Jesus. And she's become a mighty woman of God, with great gifts.

Dad and I looked at each other. He didn't know whether to laugh or cry. I thought what had happened was just mental! Gave him a high-five. And made another cup of tea.

I tell you what – those posh cakes don't half do a good job, especially around deliverance! I found out later, you see, that's what you call it: deliverance. Well, I'd always been like a postman, turning up when you least expected it! Deliverance – why that name? Maybe it's like giving birth to a new baby – you're delivered from or to . . . I'm not sure really, but I know what I saw. And we all know what happened. She's testimony to this day.

I began to see so many things I couldn't explain. Funnily enough, they only seemed to happen when I asked my pal the Holy Spirit! What *was* strange was that people started coming to me. It was like God was sending them. I believe he was, and that was daunting at first because I knew I couldn't do anything. But I could always call on my pal and he never failed. It's quite comforting to know that there's such a huge power who lives in me – and in you.

I started to look around at different churches. I didn't often see people asking the Holy Spirit to help them. The ones who did then seemed to act as if they had changed things themselves. They called on the Holy Spirit outside of them, and I didn't think that was how it should be. I felt it had to come from within.

* * *

I'd resolved to be single for the rest of my life. It seemed as if God was calling me to do things and to go places, and for that I would need to be alone.

Then I met Sarah. But not as you might imagine.

I'd helped one of my friends to get free from addiction. I'd played a part in his recovery and he was doing very well, working for drug and alcohol services. One day he phoned.

'Mick? I've got this lady with me, and she's a nice lady. She's lost her kids through drink and drugs and we can't help her here. I feel so bad about letting her go back out and I don't know what to do. You know that Jesus bloke, don't you?'

'Yeah, I do.'

'Could you ask him to help her? 'Cause I can't think of what else, you know. They've said she's a lost cause.'

'I'll ask him.'

The long and short of it is, I picked them both up. We sneaked her into my car outside drug and alcohol services and drove away. But I soon realized she was insane. I had to stop the car, and as I tried to talk to her she had her hands all over my head. She was trying to pull my earring out; she was agitated; she had the colour of death – you know, that grey colour? She was a beauty. But she was dying. And she didn't know it.

I began to raise my voice. I told her to shut her face and listen! And she did. I asked my pal the Holy Spirit to help and I began to pray for her. And in that prayer, it felt as if I was saying things I wouldn't normally have said – things that might have hurt her feelings and upset her. But they just came out my mouth. She began to cry, and I carried on praying.

Then I stopped. 'Now it's time to go.'

We drove her home and dropped her off. My friend asked me what I thought would happen.

'It's fifty-fifty. She's going to die unless she stops drinking today. She's got no chance otherwise. She's got the colour of death in her face. All bets are off. Unless she stops drinking today or tomorrow, I'll get ready to go to her funeral.' And that was that. I thought no more about it.

Six months later I was walking down the road and towards me came this lovely woman with huge, beautiful eyes and eyelashes. The light from her eyes was unbelievable. She had something so special.

'You don't remember me, Mick, do you?'

'I don't, love; I don't.'

'I'm Sarah. You prayed for me when I was in your car.'

'Oh my goodness! You look amazing.'

'Thank you.' She told me, 'I went home that day and I got down on my hands and knees and I begged God to help me. I've never drunk or taken a drug since. But I'm desperate, Mick. I've been in rehab for six months – they got me in within a week – but I *know* I'm going to drink. I just know it. Can you help me?'

I did. Through prayer, through linking her up with people, through all the things you do. And we became friends. I wonder now if I was attracted to her . . . I didn't think I was at all, yet she was so beautiful, surely I couldn't not be? Maybe God was keeping my eyes shut so I could support her a bit? I don't know, but it seemed strange.

We'd been friends for maybe two years when one evening she asked me to go with her to pray with someone. We went to the house and as we prayed, Sarah and the other lady began to cry. I just kept on praying, and after a while we left.

As I dropped Sarah off at home, I went to give her a cuddle as I must have done a thousand times before, but as I put my arms around her and she put her arms around me, oh my goodness! What was this? My heart was fluttering, I could feel butterflies in my stomach. I pulled away and grabbed the steering wheel with both hands, so my hands wouldn't touch her, even by mistake.

'Ta ra,' she said as she jumped out of the car. Her heels click-clacked all the way to the front door. I heard it open and close, and then I drove kind of erratically round the corner. *Oh no! I've got feelings for her. I've known her for years . . . What on earth?*

I got home, made myself a coffee and had a cigarette. I thought, *I can't just leave it.* So I texted: 'You know, Sarah, I'm really sorry to send this message, but when you were leaving and I put my arms round you, I felt attracted to you. And I don't know if we can be friends on that basis, but I can't lie to you. Something happened and I'm really sorry.'

And the answer came back: 'So did I, Mick; so did I.'

The conversation that followed was: 'I'll come and see you tomorrow, and let's just have a little chat.'

Morning came and I was so excited. I even had a spray of that smelly stuff, which wasn't like me at the time. If I'd had any hair, I'd have put gel on. I was experiencing teenager-like feelings that I'd heard about but never really had.

I picked her up and we went and got two coffees. We drove out of town and I pulled over in a quiet spot. The conversation wasn't good! I looked at her out of the corner of my eye – she was a stunningly beautiful woman. I'd never realized how beautiful she was. It was her eyes, you see . . . She'd made an effort as well, I could tell. She smelt really nice. She had lipstick on, but it was lipstick that sort of matched – it was dull, but beautiful.

She looked perfect.

'What are we going to do, Mick?'

'I don't know, Sarah, but I think . . .' And then it just came out my mouth. 'I think that what I should do is snog you now in the car and, if it feels all right, then you can be my girlfriend. And if it doesn't, then we'll just be mates. What d'you think?'

She looked at me. She seemed quite shocked! 'Erm . . . oh . . . yeah, all right then.'

I put my coffee down. I looked at her and I thought, *Should I close my eyes? I don't know really* . . . As I leant forward she leant forward and I nearly headbutted her! Then her eyes closed and I saw her eyelashes. I tasted her lips, just touched my tongue on hers . . . and I felt something so special. I felt like stars were fizzing inside me. I felt loved. I felt really emotional. My eyes were welling up. And as I put my arms around her and held her, I knew this was different. I'd always tried to love, but I realized that night, I'd never really let anyone love me back.

We got engaged soon afterwards and married not long ago. She's the woman who stands by my side every day. She's the rock who holds me up. You see, there's God and there's Sarah. God comes first in our relationship, but Sarah and I have been through so much together.

A week after the wedding, she had a breast removed and started chemotherapy. It ravaged her body and made her so ill. But that tingling feeling has never left. And as I've watched her recover over the last year, it's just got stronger and stronger.

You see, she became a woman of God. I told her about Jesus and I introduced her to my pal the Holy Spirit. And he's done amazing things in this woman's life.

I'm so proud to call her my wife.

* * *

With Sarah by my side, it was easier to rebuild my relationships with my children. There was much they had to forgive me for. But they did.

I became particularly close to my youngest son. Through all the badness, all the illness, all the sickness I had, my second wife had *never* stopped me seeing him. You know, when we were together, I didn't treat her the best. But she was as fine an example of motherhood as I've ever seen. She was like a lioness.

I'd pick Jack up and we'd have a chat. If she needed anything and I had it, it was hers. The relationship was good. Then the day came . . .

Jack was upstairs. She'd made me a cup of coffee, and then she told me she had cancer. She was going to fight it. I can't explain it, but I knew by what she was saying, or how she was saying it, that she was going to die. I just knew.

Over the next eighteen months, I took care to spend time preparing Jack. I watched her spiral down, through the weight loss and the treatment, and thought I'd never met a stronger person in my life. She was such a fine example to her children and to everyone around her.

And when the time came, she was ready.

A few weeks before, I'd asked her if I could pray for her, and she said, 'Yeah. I'm not really into all that, Mick, you know that, but yeah.'

I asked her a few questions and prayed, and she got some peace. And she died in peace. The undertaker came that very night. And when I walked back into the room, there was a single red rose on the pillow with a card. But the old woodchip paper on the wall looked so drab – nothing was the same now she'd gone.

What about my son? He was only seventeen. Would he come and live with me? What would become of him? The day before she died, I'd asked her to write a letter and a card for his twenty-first. And she did. I took it away and locked it in a safe.

As I write this book, only a week ago I gave Jack the letter. And the memories came flooding back.

'I love you, Dad. That letter's just like my mum!'

12
TAILOR-MADE

MY DESIRE TO UNDERSTAND GOD and to try to follow him became all-consuming. I began to wander round different churches – some with steeples, some with beautiful slates on the roof, some built out of stone with carved columns. Others were like community centres with hatches to pass through tea and coffee.

All different. With all sorts of people.

And I didn't fit in!

It wasn't that everyone spoke with long words I couldn't understand; I often had good conversations as we milled around after a service. But all the time I'd be thinking, *I'm a recovering addict.* For the moment at least, that seemed to be my identity. You know, you could ask me any question, such as, 'Is it sunny today?' and I'd reply, 'It is. Did you know I'm a recovering addict?' 'Oh yeah, would you like a cup of tea?' 'Yes, I'm a recovering addict!'

I think I was proud to be getting free and I just wanted everyone else to appreciate the progress I was making, but that blinded me to other people's needs. Yet there was definitely a language these Christian people spoke that I didn't know. I felt they had a secret I wasn't allowed into – I was being kept at arm's length. For instance, in many places you could only pray if you were part of the prayer team.

The bands were good and looked really professional – all those beautiful, tanned people. When I went to one church with a pointy steeple, I noticed the priest seemed to do everything himself. I wondered, *Why is he up there?* I felt . . . separate. He had very fancy clothes and the bright colours made me think of *Joseph and the Amazing Technicolor Dreamcoat*. (Or sometimes: 'My grandma used to wear a dress like that!')

Lots of nice people, everywhere I went. But I felt an outsider. And I wasn't sure why.

* * *

I ended up in a Christian college. On a degree course! Though I hadn't managed to become part of a church, my thirst for knowledge just kept growing. Within twelve months, however, it became apparent that I wasn't going to pass. The percentages I was getting were ridiculously poor and I was heading for failure.

At this point, someone suggested that I might have educational problems. So I went for a test and discovered that I had profound dyslexia, dyspraxia and Irlen syndrome. Now all that sounds very posh, but what it means is that I couldn't read or write or retain information. And light was distorted in my eyes.

I never knew! .

I thought back to when I was a child . . . the teacher standing me on the table and forcing me to make noises like a donkey, 'Hee-haw, hee-haw', because I was stupid. She was wrong. I wasn't stupid after all – I had an illness. It was such a relief to find out, and I felt a real peace.

Pretty soon, I was given a coloured overlay to put over words. That helped a little but not a lot, so I began to save as much as I could for some special glasses to improve my vision.

Finally, they arrived, tailor-made for me, tinted. I put them on and picked up a book, and all the letters and all the words went still. How can I describe it? Well . . . you know when you have dirty windows in your house and as the sun shines on them you can see all the streaks and marks everywhere? It was like they'd been cleaned! Crisp. Clear. Sparkling.

I could read! I felt tears in my eyes. It was such a revelation to me. I began to read everything I possibly could. I was reading the back of packets of cornflakes. I was reading sauce bottles – anything and everything. I felt like I had a new lease of life.

I picked up the Bible and began to read that. What a joy!

I did fail my first year, but I took it again. My studies lasted four years instead of three, but I qualified with a very good degree. How extraordinary is that?!

But with God, all things are possible.

My time at university really shaped me. I came to understand Jesus in a new and profound way. Things were painful at times, but growth seems to be like that. I managed to stay sober and clean from drugs through all the frustrations and tried to trust God at every turn, but I found myself homeless, down on my luck and sleeping in my car. I was still doing my studies. How could this be? An (almost) ex-drug addict trying to do a degree in theology, living in the back of his car. But that's how it was.

And then one day my phone rang. It was the principal of the college: 'Are you sleeping in your car, Mick?'

'I might be.'

'Come and see me.'

There were very few words exchanged. She just took me to a room on the campus. I'll never forget it – it smelt so clean and fresh. It had a little shower room, a bed. It had a cupboard and a wardrobe, a desk, a chair and a mirror. I remember looking in that mirror and thinking, *I've been in places like this before. But this is different. This institution is different.*

There were folded-up towels on the bed, all clean. Fresh bedding.

'Right, Mick,' she said, 'you can live here.'

I was stunned. I looked at her face and it was soft, her eyes so kind. You know, if she'd been a stick of rock and you'd snapped her in half, you would have read LOVE in the middle. I wasn't like that. I felt I was a Christian, a believer in Jesus. But I wasn't like that.

'Have you any money, Mick?'

'I don't, no.'

'Wait there.' She went away and came back with food. She'd gone to the shop and bought everything I needed. She left it with me and walked out with a smile.

I sat on the bed and put my head in my hands. I could feel my fingers just above my eyebrows, my thumb running across the bridge of my nose. Tears again. This woman didn't really know me. And I didn't have what she had.

Within a few days, there had been a bit of a disaster on the campus; a floor had collapsed. I had some skills – I had learnt some things in my time over the years! – so I offered to mend the floor. I spent two weeks working on it for free, because they were looking after me, these people. They'd offered me a home and food. And after I'd repaired the floor, they gave me a job that allowed me to pay for my room and for my own food.

I started to feel empowered. I was working part-time and studying with fresh enthusiasm. I picked a book up and I read about a fella called John Wesley. I thought, *I'm like him, except he's a lot cleverer than me.* You see, this John Wesley believed in his head, but he didn't believe in his heart. He wasn't certain. He still had doubt. I was like him.

But as I read on, I discovered he had a moment – a moment when he came to accept Jesus fully in his heart. He was changed and transformed, just like the lady who had given me the room and the food parcel.

I wasn't like them. But I wanted to be. I *needed* to be. I wanted to grasp what they had.

There was a chaplain on the campus, a lovely lady, very softly spoken. I asked if I could see her and she agreed. Sitting in her office I said, 'You know, I've come to this college, and all these people here are talking about being saved. And they talk about all these different things, and I don't understand any of it. Jesus died on the cross for my sins. I want to think I know what that means. I've been trying to follow Jesus, but it's nearly impossible – it's so hard!'

A gentle touch on the shoulder to stop me.

'What does it mean to be saved?' I asked.

She looked me full in the face. She was another one of those soft-skinned people with beautiful eyes that were so alive. 'Mick, he died especially for you. And he wants you to accept that.'

Something happened. I began to choke. I began to sob. How could he love *me*? After everything I'd done?

She just said it again. '*Especially* you, Mick. God's going to be with you. He's got great plans for you.'

That's when I broke. I physically felt my heart soften. What I wanted so badly was really happening! It seemed as if my heart had been like a brick, but now, if you squeezed it, it would have been like a sponge. I wanted it to soak in as much love as possible. I took a deep breath and felt as if I was breathing in warm air. I felt as if my lungs were being purified. I felt sinless . . . in that moment.

From then on, *everything* changed.

Everything!

* * *

I'd met an older couple who invited me to their home regularly. I would stay over sometimes, and they'd feed me, look after me and speak to me constantly about Jesus. They were soft-skinned, beautiful-eyed people as well. They became like a mother and father to me and I love them dearly. Having seen me struggle, they lifted me up, got alongside me and spoke life into my world. Even to this day, they support my ministry.

You see, after I'd become born again, things began to get a bit funky. I started to see so many strange happenings, unlike any I'd ever witnessed before. My friends began to write these incidents down, and I'm so glad to have their record of them. Some will be mentioned in this book, and others I'll share at a later date. Looking back, many were so profound that – being only human – I still find it difficult to come to terms with them. I'd begun viewing the world in a different way, and fear simply wasn't there. I remember thinking, *Have* I *turned into one of those soft-skinned people?* I wasn't sure – I wasn't sure at all.

In the midst of all the happenings, I was carrying on with my studies. It seems almost selfish as I say it, but I needed some reassurance that I was going in the right direction. So I prayed for a sign from God. I went to bed one night asking for a revelation, or for anything at all – I was clutching at straws! I was studying as hard as I could and I didn't want it to be all for nothing.

The next morning, I walked out of my room and into the familiar kitchen. I opened my eyes, and what I saw turned my world upside down.

I looked at the kettle, the white kettle, and there was every colour of the rainbow radiating from it. I looked at the fridge; it was the same. The teaspoon I took out of the drawer was like a spoon but fifteen times wider, because all the colours of the rainbow were wrapped around it! *Everything* was radiating light.

I looked out the window at the trees in the garden. They were just so beautiful. Every leaf was coloured and irradiated round the edges. The bark of the tree was alive! My eye was caught by a man and his dog, and I felt as if I'd seen into a different realm. There were two multicoloured lights – a tall one and a small one – walking along a multicoloured pavement!

A huge smile spread over my face, but the adrenalin was pumping, pumping. I couldn't make a coffee. I couldn't do it. I sat down at the table in the dining room and looked at the salt and pepper pots. As I reached out to touch them, I saw my hand was radiating the same light. Every part of my body was glowing with this multicoloured madness!

I closed my eyes and fell into prayer: 'Lord, thank you so much. I must be going in the right direction.'

Back in the kitchen again, I turned the tap on. Multicoloured water sprayed and bounced everywhere – beads and beams of light and colour. I splashed it on to my face and on to my eyes. I opened them again, but the colour was only getting stronger and stronger. The euphoria was fading and I was beginning to feel afraid. What if I was stuck with this for the rest of my life? What if I could never see normally again?

I went back to prayer. 'Thank you, Lord, for everything you're doing for me. Thank you for guiding me and granting me this beautiful vision and reassuring me we're going in the right direction. But Lord, please take it away.'

I opened my eyes and everything was as usual. And then I felt sorrowful and guilty. But I'd experienced something that was very real to me. From that moment on, I had no doubt that God would lead me wherever he wanted me to be. And although it wouldn't be easy, I'd follow him. I'd push through anything.

You see, I've seen the world in a different light – literally!

* * *

There would be many more extraordinary happenings along the way. I was often almost without money, but then money would appear – every single time. For *everything* I needed.

There was an incident when a letter came through the post to the college and it was a fine for £40 for driving in a bus lane. Oh, man! I'm not from the big city. I didn't know about bus lanes (though I definitely knew about fines – I'd had a few of them in my time). I felt very disappointed, because money was tight, and yet the penalty had to be paid.

Later in the car with a friend, heading into the village to get some lunch, I said, 'I can't believe it. Have you seen this?' and I showed him a picture of my car. 'No blagging. Done. Forty quid. I don't know what to do.'

'Well, have you asked God?'

'No . . . but what am I going to do? You can't not pay it, can you? And I can't pretend it's not me. It's the registration – there's a picture of the car!

'But I will.'

So I pulled over to the side of the road and said, 'Lord, I'm really sorry. I didn't know that I was driving in a bus lane. Jesus, you know I'm skint. Holy Spirit, can you help me out? And thank you, Father, in Jesus' name. Ame—' I hadn't finished the 'n' in 'Amen' when a van ran right into the back of the car. I looked at my friend.

He smiled. 'Not the best of days, Mick, is it?'

'No.' I got out. There was a lady delivering parcels. And she was so apologetic, I didn't have the heart even to take her insurance details. When I looked, there wasn't really any damage to either vehicle – just a dint. It was absolutely fine, but she insisted – she put her hand in her purse and pressed some money into my hand. Then drove away.

I got back in the car in shock. And when I opened my hand, there was £50: £40 to cover the fine, and £5 each for lunch.

'Thank you, Jesus. A very quick answer.'

My friend was in tears of laughter, and he said those words I'd heard before many times but simply not understood: 'God's surely with you, Mick. He's surely with you!'

13
McDONALD'S REVISITED

THE SUPERNATURAL WAS BEGINNING to become something I just expected to happen. And that has really been the pattern of my Christian walk. The things that occurred weren't what I was particularly begging for, or wanting, or needing, but they were miraculous. God seems to have kept me going at every turn. I think it would be true to say he keeps supplying everything I need.

One day, I got a phone call from a friend of mine from the past: 'Mick, you believe in that Jesus geezer, don't you?'

'I do, yeah.'

'Can you say a prayer for one of me mates? I'm out of town and I just can't get to him. He's said he's going to kill himself, and I think he will. There's nothing I can do. I've rung round and there's nobody to go and help him . . . and I suppose nobody can stop him.'

I said, 'Yeah, I'll pray for him, I'll ask Jesus. But can you send me his address or his phone number or something?'

'Yeah, I will, I will, Mick.'

He texted me the address and his mate's name and I began to pray. Sitting in my room, I tried to imagine what he looked like and how he'd kill himself – what he'd do. I asked, 'How do we stop him, Jesus?' And then I said, 'Please just give me a chance to speak to him and tell him about you.' I looked at the address and it was half an hour's drive away. Petrol was low and money was tight, but I knew Jesus wanted me to go.

So that's what I did. I got into the car and set off. I found the house on a nice terraced street, then parked, not quite outside, but two or three houses down. As I walked up, checking and double-checking the number on the door, I noticed there was a gap between the curtains – not very big but enough to peer through. And I saw him. He was standing on a chair that didn't look too stable; hanging from the ceiling rose was a rope. He was putting his head in it.

I decided I wouldn't knock on the window – I'd go for the door handle. It turned easily and I walked straight in, opened the door on the right-hand side and entered the room where he was standing. 'Come down. Jesus has sent me.'

He took the rope off. He almost fell off the chair! I remember he was wearing a white T-shirt with writing right down the front of it at an angle, and he was dripping wet with sweat. A young man, no more than twenty-eight or twenty-nine years of age. Desperate.

We sat down and he told me the story of his past – the suffering he'd been through. The state of his mental health was poor.

'How did you know? How did you know?'

'How do you mean?'

'I just said a prayer. I said, "God, if you don't want me to die, send somebody."'

I felt so . . . humble? I still didn't really know what humble felt like, but God had used me. I wasn't worthy – and yet I was! The young man saw it as a miracle. I saw it as a soul saved and I prayed with him. I had a cross around my neck on a chain. I took it off and gave it to him.

'Will this protect me?'

'Well, the cross will, because that's Jesus. And he's everywhere, in everything. All you have to do is follow him.'

I left him my number and drove away. The young man lived. He'd called out to God, and God had stepped in.

On the motorway, the lights seemed to be going at a hundred miles an hour, flaring and flickering by. It was almost as if I was seeing my life flash before me. I remember reading something at college by one of those really clever people, a guy called Dietrich Bonhoeffer. He said, 'When God calls a man, he calls him to die.' And Bonhoeffer had given his life for Christ. I thought, *Would I?* I didn't know was the answer, but it felt possible. It felt as if I probably would. Yeah, I probably would.

When I went to bed that night, I thought again about all the times people had said to me, 'God's with you, Mick!', 'God's surely with you, Mick!', 'Mick, God is with you!', and I believed it. Probably for the first time in my life I *believed* it. There was a sense of purpose growing in me.

* * *

I was enjoying my weekends now. I'd go and spend time with Dad, take him out somewhere, before we inevitably ended up in a coffee shop. We'd talk about the football, or God, or music – we both loved Irish music. When we played songs like 'The Fields of Athenry', he would recall how his dad used to tap dance in the pub on a tin sheet and people would throw pennies at him – they were fascinated! I learned that he had committed suicide. He'd become an alcoholic, you see, because he couldn't cope with what he'd seen and been through in the First World War. My grandmother was left with four children to bring up alone. Those were tough days and tough times – impoverished, but very moralistic.

The conversations with my dad in the final years of his life were amazing and revealing. I heard about the day he found a wallet with over a hundred pounds in it. A hundred pounds when he was ten years of age was enough to buy a house! He didn't manage to spend even ten bob of it (fifty pence in today's money), though it wasn't for lack of trying. He bought everything he could think of but could hardly get through any of it at all. Then his mum discovered what had happened, and she had to scrimp and save to repay the missing cash. She was a devout Catholic. Dad told me she'd never let her dead husband's name be mentioned, because, she said, he died like a dog and he was in hell.

I felt so sad. Poor woman, having to carry so much bitterness as well as pain. My dad, on the other hand, had come to terms with life. He'd found some peace after losing my mum, and he'd been reconciled with me. We loved each other; we were men together.

On the day of his ninetieth birthday, he was taken ill and hospitalized. The nurse told me that he would live for at least another three months, though she thought he must be in excruciating pain. But my dad told me: not a bit of it! He had no pain at all! And he said, 'I'll be having me dinner with your mum today!'

'No, Dad, you know you've got months left – the nurse told me.'

'Don't listen to nurses, son – that's always been your problem. Listen to God. I'm having me dinner with your mum.'

And he did. He died in peace. He just slipped away.

I didn't have the same feelings I felt when my mother died. I didn't feel joyful, but I was happy he wasn't in pain. He was with God. He'd run the race. He'd gone home.

My life would change again. My weekends would look very different. You see, nothing ever stays the same. Except God. If we trust in him, we can get through anything.

* * *

After my dad had passed away, I felt at a bit of a loss. I had so much more time on my hands and I didn't really know what to do with it. Little did I know the ministry I'm now in was about to be born.

Church on the Street came about when I decided to sit on the ground outside McDonald's with a suitcase of clothes, tea and coffee in flasks, and sandwiches, and a packet of cigarettes in my pocket. Beforehand, as I was walking up the hill at the side of the restaurant, I felt pretty apprehensive. I imagined people thinking, 'Who is this nutcase? What on earth is he doing?' But I pushed through the fear and did it anyway.

I settled myself down next to a guy who was begging and, as we talked, I opened up my suitcase and shared a brew with him. Then I fished out a sandwich and ripped it in half. I thought, *This isn't a bad way of doing communion! Nice cup of coffee and half a sandwich each.* It felt really good. I told him a little bit about my life and he told me about his, and we felt equal. That's something I've noticed churches don't do very well – they don't treat people as equals. They think they do, but when you stand back and watch, they definitely don't.

Pretty soon, there were fifty or sixty people gathering twice a week outside McDonald's. I met a husband and wife, David and Mary, who were ex-Salvation Army. They were a fantastic couple, and their heart for the ministry helped set it on fire. As they supported me and things became a little more solid and organized, we'd pray with people on the street. Christians from other churches started to come along and some of them would bake cakes. Others gave sandwiches, and before long we'd people fetching clothes too. The ministry was growing rapidly.

I felt I needed a cross and somebody made one. I still have it to this day. It folded up so I could put it in my suitcase, and whenever we met, I'd strap it to a tree.

At this point, I'd finished college but I was still employed there for two days a week. I really wanted to spend all my time on the ministry, but you've got to work, you've got to wait on God. As I did that, I reflected on some of the miracles Jesus did, and it kept coming back to this: it's all about God's timing. The supernatural is *only* about God's timing.

If when Jesus shouted, 'Lazarus, come out the tomb!' Lazarus hadn't actually come out for eighteen months, his resurrection from the dead would still have been miraculous, but it wouldn't have had quite the same effect. When Jesus commands something and it happens, it's supernatural.

And when we can share in that, that's something very special. You see, I really believe God can do anything, through Jesus Christ. And if we ask and call upon him with the power of love that's inside us, then it will happen.

Let me tell you about one day I was outside McDonald's, just giving people sandwiches and, as I like to do, having one myself to be companionable. (This means I tend to eat quite a bit!) I'm talking to a guy and there's another guy sitting a little way away, and many, many others.

Suddenly – a bang!

Silence.

Then panic, urgency. One of the lads has fallen off a bench and hit the ground. It very much looks like an overdose. People stand around as I go over and check his pulse, but I can't seem to find one and his lips are blue. I'm not medically trained; I'm not sure what to do. Just then, a first aider walks by, and he comes and takes over and tries to revive him, but no joy. We hear the wail of the ambulance as the paramedics arrive, and they do their best to bring him back to life.

But it all seems hopeless. One said, 'If you believe in God, I'd pray for him now, 'cause he's gone.' He'd noticed the cross – the cross that was strapped to the tree, right next to where my friend had fallen. You could see the anxiety in people's faces. There were tears in David's eyes, he felt so distraught. David had a wonderful depth of compassion.

I asked people to pray. And some of those standing nearby did begin to do so; I could see heads bowed. I put my hand on the lad and said simply, 'Lord, just give him a squeeze; give him a touch, Lord. Just give him one more chance. Give him another chance at life, Lord.'

Colour started to come back into his lips! His eyes were shut and there was still no pulse. But then, a sound . . . I looked up and saw people's faces begin to change. A coughing and a spluttering! We all shouted to the paramedics, who'd gone to get a body bag, and they came running over. They rushed him into the ambulance. They had to work on him, but he came back. *He came back!*

Now, the supernatural is all in God's timing. I've asked these questions many times over the years: did he just have a really faint pulse? Did it happen to be, when I prayed, that he was reviving anyway? Or was God answering my prayers?

I don't think it really matters, because he lived! He was given another chance.

And I see him most days. I wish I could say there was a really happy ending to this story – that he found Jesus; that he doesn't take drugs or drink; that he wears very nice clean clothes and doesn't sleep outside, in parks and in carparks.

But I can't.

What I can say is, *he's saved*! He has a faith like I don't see in many people. He still sleeps rough. He still drinks heavily. He still takes drugs.

But he's saved.

He told me one day that he could hear me when he was lying on the ground. He felt he had a choice, and he decided to come back because somebody cared. And it makes me wonder about the love in us that reflects the love of Jesus to others; the love in us that shines out because we have Jesus within – what *power* there must be in it! You see, it's *that* which raises people back to life.

I'm not sure to this day whether my friend rose from the dead, but I know Jesus restored him and gave him a faith. And a testimony that he uses all the time.

You see, it's not always about what others believe. In this case, it's about what he believes. And he's certain that God raised him. The rest is none of my business.

* * *

I knew I was called to ministry. I could see there were extraordinary things happening around me. And I was certain that I needed a spiritual covering so I would be accountable to someone in authority. But as I began to look at all the different denominations, I became more and more disheartened. You see, I know if an alcoholic doesn't get a drink, he can suffer an alcoholic fit – his body goes into shock and he may die. I've seen it happen right in front of my eyes. And the denominations I was looking at completely misunderstood alcoholism and its serious effects. They wouldn't support me administering alcohol, not even to the dying, but I needed to be able to do that, so it was an issue. There were many other aspects that disappointed me too and I thought I'd never find a place to rest my head. The church that I really wanted to be part of didn't seem to exist . . .

But in the meantime I graduated! It was such an exciting day. My sisters and children were there, and so proud of me. When they called my name and everybody clapped, and I stepped forward in my funny flat hat and gown and the coloured thing around my neck, I felt quite proud myself! I believed God had done something in me, because here I was, walking away with a BA Honours degree in Theology. What I would do with it I had no idea. I didn't dare to dream. I felt this was going to be a time to sit and wait. And that's what I did. I sat and I waited.

One day in church I came across a visiting bishop. He had something different about him, and when he said, 'I hate religion!' my ears pricked up. I did wonder why he wore a purple shirt and not a black one, but he talked sense.

You see, when I was studying and reading my Bible, I felt I believed what the word said. I felt the story it told was real. Yet many of my friends didn't respond this way. They didn't seem to believe in the miraculous, or that God did things now, just as he used to. But I did. And so did this bishop. He spoke my kind of language.

At the end of the meeting, I went to find Mr Purple Shirt. I shook his hand and asked him many questions. I told him I'd just finished a Theology degree and I felt called to ministry but wasn't clear quite what that might be. I was looking for someone to mentor me and to point me in the right direction. We already had the ministry on the street and it was growing, but I still needed guidance; I needed to feel accountable. I felt that with all the things I'd done and the criminal lifestyle I'd led, I should be under authority.

Bishop Steven invited me to his house. He told me about ordination and explained all the steps involved in that. And he prayed for me. It was deeply moving, and when he put his hand on my shoulder I felt that something was happening. He seemed the kind of man I could get into a boxing ring with and spar with. We'd show each other moves, but we wouldn't hit. You don't meet many people like that – a brother who you can spar with.

He made me an offer. The offer was that he would mentor me and we would meet regularly; I would have to fill out some forms and fulfil various criteria, and then, over a long period of time, he would seek to discern if I was suitable for ordination. If I was, I'd be ordained.

I kept on asking questions – around addiction, around service, around how I understood the gospel.

And he answered in a way that brought real joy to me: 'But how you understand it *is* the gospel, Mick! What you're telling people is the truth. And of course we'll support you in sharing that.'

I began to feel a fresh excitement, and that gave me the energy to put time and effort into building the ministry and into doing a little bit more study and research to help me move towards ordination.

It was in one of my regular meetings with Bishop Steven that he discerned I was afraid to have money and he asked me why. I paused for a moment. I looked into his kind eyes and I said, 'It's because I've been so destructive when I've had it.'

His response was, 'Yes, but that's because money had power over you. We need to pray about that, because how can you build a ministry when you have no money and you're not even able to accept it?'

So we prayed. And as we prayed, in my mind I heard a break. You know when someone's in a forest and they stumble on a twig and it cracks and the noise sort of echoes around? It was just like that. I didn't suddenly develop an ambition to be rich, but I gradually came to an understanding that God would provide for me – if I accepted his provision. And I would be able to build the ministry and serve the poor, all the time listening to God.

I spoke to David and Mary about all of this, and David affirmed my understanding and said he really felt that God would always provide, *always* provide, if we followed his way.

The week before my ordination, Bishop Steven prayed for me again. I'd never had anybody prophesy over me before – ever. I'd had people say 'God is with you, Mick', as you know, but this was different. Bishop Steven told me that the ministry would grow very quickly. He said things like, 'There will be TV. There will be books. There will be big money you'll have to handle, and big responsibility you'll have to shoulder. And God will be with you in every step that you take. This is what's going to happen. This is what's waiting for you, should you choose to receive what God has for you. Be ready. He's with you.' Bishop Steven told me how he would support me in all this.

To be honest, I kind of dismissed what he'd said – the rantings of a crazy man? Surely such things couldn't happen for me? It was just a bishop being nice to someone who's about to be ordained. Or perhaps this was a real word from God?

The day of my ordination arrived. And as the service went on, with my family and various dignitaries, including the mayor, politicians and the local MP, all watching, I felt I was . . . not a fraud exactly. I felt I was unworthy. But as the bishop laid hands on me and prayed, something exploded inside. Remember when you were a child and you packed wet sand into a bucket and you pushed it and pushed it and made it so tight, then it dried and all at once, wooosh!? Well, that was the effect I experienced *everywhere* in my body – even in my mind and my thoughts and my breath. I was alive!

I looked at the bishop in his pointy hat and long robes, and I felt . . . loved. I think he's a little bit younger than me, but he felt like my father. I trust him. I know he cares. I walked away from my ordination with a new assurance. I was able to stand tall, with my shoulders back. I knew that God was with me and I was under authority, something that to this day I think is very important for us all. We need someone we can be accountable to.

I started wearing a black shirt and a dog collar. I decided that if it helped me preach the gospel and tell people about Jesus, then I'd always wear it. And if it didn't, then I wouldn't. But very quickly I found that many more people than before were coming to me and telling me about their problems, and letting me know about opportunities to pray with others. So I dress in black with a light dog collar. Those clothes have become part of who I am.

Within a short period of time, we found a community centre. You know those places with a hatch to pass tea and coffee through? One like that! All the people who were turning up on the street needed a home, and for £20 for a Sunday afternoon, we had our very own church.

It grew very quickly, and before you knew it, there were eighty to ninety people turning up every week. As the minister taking the service, I remember one day standing at the front speaking into a microphone and thinking, *How miraculous is this! This could only be God.*

You see, God uses the foolish to confound the wise. That's what he did with me. He took a fool and put him in a position of authority and, I have to say, a lot of the wise didn't like it. That became a real big disappointment to me, because I simply wasn't mature enough to handle it emotionally. I began to feel down and depressed. I was just trying to do the best I could, and people at other churches were saying things like, 'You aren't a proper church because you're in a little rented building.' But I just decided to trust God. And to push on.

David and Mary, Sarah and I – we prayed. We prayed and prayed and prayed! There were times when I'd sit in David and Mary's house and pray with them till the early hours of the morning. We prayed for Burnley, and for the town to receive salvation, and for people to come to know Jesus like never before. We believed. We trusted. We put the effort in. We made a decision that we would not stop.

Within no time at all, the pandemic was on the horizon.

David sadly passed away.

And everything changed again.

14
DROPPING OFF THE MERCHANDISE

I WAS SITTING IN A CAFÉ with a coffee in my hand, just kind of stroking my face with it and slurping quietly while my mind doodled and wandered about. There were pictures on the wall saying something like '50p off your next cappuccino when you buy 3,000 brews in here and get your card stamped!' and highly magnified photos of bacon sandwiches that looked nothing like the real deal I'd just bought. The hard plastic chair had me kind of twisting and turning, my back aching, but the bacon sandwich tasted beautiful.

I looked up, and there in front of me, a tall dark figure, a Crombie, undone, black. I could just about see the shoes. They weren't shiny. They were slightly dull, working shoes – that's what I would call them. Not too clean, but not filthy. Proper working shoes.

As I raised my eyes, I took in a black shirt. And a lovely dog collar. I almost felt a little bit inferior! I felt my hand go instinctively to my throat and my eight quid's worth of shirt and collar as I looked at probably eighty quid's worth. His face was soft, but he wasn't like one of those Christians I'd become accustomed to. He was very real. He didn't look as if he'd had the type of life I'd had, but there were definitely stories in those eyes. There was a genuine warmth about him.

I remember he flicked his hair and ran his fingers through it to smooth it back to the side. He touched his glasses as he spoke to me, and he put his hand out. 'Father Alex, St Matthew's Church.'

'Pleased to meet you, Father Alex. I'm Pastor Mick from . . . church on the street, because that's where my church is, I guess!'

'Pleased to meet you.'

We went on to become friends. We'd have interaction in small ways. He was a Church of England vicar and a nice guy, you know? A nice guy. I like Father Alex. He just has . . . well, you don't really know what it is or how to describe it, but it's something. Father Alex has got that in abundance.

About a year later, I undertook a little retreat. It was just before the first lockdown. It was as if we knew something was coming, although we didn't know what it looked like or how it would play out. But things were about to change – that would become so obvious.

I went away to pray. I only stayed over at the retreat centre for one night. The church was paying for it for me – I think it was about £80 at the time – and I felt guilty taking the money. But I did, nonetheless. I took it. And when I prayed, I felt as if it was time . . . you know, like, *my* time. Almost as if I'd been born for this time. I didn't know what that meant, but I was certainly going to find out.

Within weeks, the lockdown had been imposed and the streets became deserted.

There was never any question of me staying put in my house. I'd have been like a caged lion – it just wasn't going to happen! I realized the way out was to: one, serve God and, two, do as much as I could to bring Jesus to the people. As times got tougher, with supermarkets either closed or having only limited opening hours, many were feeling sort of lost. I had to help. We'd been feeding people on the street, and we'd been told that wasn't allowed any more. But I couldn't take that on board. I wouldn't take no for an answer.

I remember having a cup of coffee at home and thinking, *What am I going to do?* And as I continued thinking and praying, after a while I felt this new resolve. I got a pen and a piece of paper and split the town up into four. I decided I was going to get food together, sandwiches and things that could be heated up, and I was going to take it to people, or at least drop it, where they could pick it up. Even better, if I could, would be to meet and engage with people. The food would all be packaged – I wouldn't have touched it. I felt it was dreadful that human touch had been taken away; it just couldn't be right – this fear we suddenly had of being in contact with one another. I really didn't feel anxious about that. But I knew I had to follow the rules.

And then, sitting in my kitchen, I had another thought. *I've been a criminal all my life and I've got this huge desire to serve people and to serve God. How am I going to do it?*

The answer was so clear: 'Do what you've always done.'

And that was it. That was it.

I went to see Father Alex. The community centre where we'd been meeting only gave us access for one hour on a Sunday, but Father Alex had a church. After a conversation, we decided to set a foodbank up there. And I organized it exactly as I would have when I was living a criminal life.

So, if you can imagine . . . What you do is you get people to drop off merchandise in a certain area. Then you collect it and get people to come in and bag it all up. Then you take it out and deliver it. Now that may be what *you* call drug dealing. But that's what *I* call redemption!

Father Alex's church became a central collection point, and he and I began delivering food parcels in my small Toyota Aygo. Such a tiny little car! We would find ourselves in tears as it got packed to the brim over and over again. You see, the foodbank we set up had a huge impact on us emotionally, as well as in other ways. God was using us and blessing our churches, and the community was pulling together and supporting us in our work. The amount of food arriving became off the scale – it ran into thousands and thousands of pounds' worth. We delivered thousands and thousands of parcels!

When we used a van, I would do the dropping off. One particular afternoon, I found myself about to visit a house, and there was something about the space between the garden gate and the front door that made me wonder about Jesus – about how he might stand there on the path between the two. People had become so afraid, they wouldn't interact, they felt they just couldn't, and they wouldn't let anyone in their home. It was a scary time.

I knocked on the door and it opened. A young man. I gave him the food parcel and he said, 'Do you want to come in, Mick?'

'Yeah.' And I did. I don't know whether I'm ashamed to admit this or not, but I didn't follow the lockdown rules too well. That may be right and it may be wrong, but it's the truth.

I sat in this lad's house and he told me he was feeling suicidal. He shared lots of other things about his drug use and his life, and I told him about mine. It became a regular thing. He was such a nice lad but just a little bit lost, and like that other exceptional young man I'd encountered in the psychiatric unit, a lovely human being.

I met many people whose mental health had spiralled down, and some of them would invite me in because they were just so desperate. We delivered food parcels on one street to three young men, in different houses, who all took their own lives. At that point I knew that the price of the pandemic would be heavy – so heavy. I was going into houses where children were sitting on the floor in their pyjamas and dressing gowns with a packet of Rice Krispies, and they were eating straight from the box because that's all they had.

I cried a lot in those days. I'd been doing this work for ten years, but now I saw poverty in a different light. It was increasing because it was wrapped around with fear. People didn't know what they were going to do. They were dying, and not just of COVID – they were dying of being unloved.

The world had locked its door. Covered its face.

And the churches had slammed the doors and bolted them shut.

I really felt this couldn't be right, and I started doing church services out in carparks and on the streets. People began to turn up. I remember on one occasion, when it was a little bit iffy because you weren't sure what you could and what you couldn't do, I was in a carpark across from Tesco's. I'd heard a whisper that during a pandemic you can't stop food distribution. So it might be all right to turn up with a van full of food on Sunday, as long as I had a health and safety plan on the front seat of the van? I think I may have made it up in my head! Nevertheless, it was written down.

I had a little speaker and a microphone, and I'd preach and talk about Jesus.

I wondered, *Where's the best place to do it? How can I make this work?* Don't get me wrong, I wasn't without fear, but I knew I was going to do it anyway and I thought the best place would be right next to the police station!

So that's where I set up the church – Church on the Street – right next to the police station. I got away with it for about two weeks. Then the police landed. It was like *The Sweeney* and *The Flying Squad* with all those sirens going; such a shock. My heart was really beating fast. They blocked the carpark and people began to scatter. A lot of my parishioners were not entirely law-abiding, so when they saw a blue light, they were off! You could hear the words 'Leg it!' and shoe leather pounding up the street!

The policemen came straight over. 'What's your name? What are you doing?'

I noticed one in particular. He was desperate to arrest me. He was a big guy, a stocky guy, with dark eyes and dark hair. He had a stab vest on – well, obviously you need that when you go to arrest a priest – and he looked me full in the face. 'What you doing? It's illegal, you're causing a disturbance, you're killing people . . .'

Wow!

I opened the back of the van and showed him all the food. I gave him the 'risk assessment' card. And I could overhear his conversation on the radio: 'Yeah, but . . . No, I know, but . . .' It seemed someone at the other end was advising him to leave me alone.

As I waited to see whether I would be locked up for the day, or just given a colossal fine, I saw Gordon, who'd so kindly taken me into his home all those years ago. And he was praying with the other policemen! He had his hand on the shoulder of one, and I felt this real peace.

Well, my friend was not happy. There was a frown, there was anger. His hair seemed to have got extra spiky and his tanned skin was beginning to crease. He was not happy at all.

But the police got back into their vans and off they went, no sirens.

As they left, I picked up the microphone once again and I played 'Amazing Grace', turning the volume up full. The music hovered above us, filling the air. I heard a little bit of sniffling, and when I looked close, I could see many people were in tears . . . Church on the Street was alive. Even the police were leaving us alone. We'd found a way to do church when all the others were closed. I thank God to this day that our doors were never bolted.

You see, you can't put the Holy Spirit in a box.

Over the next few weeks, we saw more and more people gathering in the carpark on Sundays. I began to feel a little anxious when we were doing the services, because the more people who were there, it seemed, the greater the risk. However, we split people into groups in the carparking bays and did everything as safely as we could. We even had marshals. And some people would drive past and give us a toot and wave. But there were others who would shout at us and call us murderers.

Such strange, strange times.

I remember delivering food down empty roads, empty streets; talking to old people who daren't come to the door but were so glad to have someone to speak to through the window. I think in the first twelve months of the pandemic, humanity lost its spark. People were dying spiritually. So much of life that we'd taken for granted was being lost.

Coming together on Saturday mornings with Father Alex at his church, to give out food and receive what was coming in, became something of a highlight for me. People were making their way from all over the place to help. It was such a joy, and we found ourselves deeply moved, week after week. I'd witnessed extreme poverty all my life, but I don't think Father Alex had seen it quite like I had, and his reaction brought out the best in me.

You see, I believe if politicians and church leaders could only weep *with* the poor, then things would change. Father Alex and I would regularly weep together, with and for the poor. This is something very, very special because it allows you to see that the good news for the poor is for us. *We* are the poor. It's not them after all. It's us.

That's what I got from being with Father Alex. I found a brotherhood and a peace with him that allowed me to be who I really was. He helped me to cry. And for that I'll forever be grateful.

* * *

One day we got a call from the BBC. They wanted to come and see Father Alex and me about the possibility of doing an item for the news. The two of us discussed it, and we thought, yeah, why not? What harm can it do?

So we had a meeting with these guys from the BBC. I vividly remember the first time I met them: it soon became clear that they were three good people, three honest people. Encountering Ed Thomas in particular, the BBC's Special

Correspondent for the News, was going to change my life, though funnily enough, at first I didn't really trust him! I didn't know much about journalists and I was on my guard. I think he had to work hard to gain my confidence.

The team just followed us round. Father Alex and I had our separate ministries, so sometimes we'd be on our own and sometimes we'd be together. Phil, the cameraman, a Scouser (from Liverpool!), was really down to earth. I felt a brotherly kind of connection with him. I felt we were equals. He seemed to understand how I felt. As for Ed, he looked as if he should be in a boy band but he was about ten years too late. Very smart. Very well spoken. Cropped hair. He was like a throwback, you know? Not rock 'n' roll as such, but nice rock 'n' roll. That's what Ed looked like. He was rock 'n' roll without the bad language. And then there was the lady who was the producer, Louise. She'd always be checking to make sure everything was all right, that we were okay and that things were coming together.

Father Alex and I were quite bemused – we had no idea what they were talking about and (to be frank) no idea what we were doing. We'd look at each other and say 'Cut!' and laugh. But they captured a moment in time. The things that we thought were normal, even though we struggled with them, weren't normal. We'd become accustomed to the poverty we were seeking to alleviate. I don't think we'd become acclimatized to it, but we'd become accustomed.

They filmed me unloading food in the carpark, where so many people were coming during the pandemic. In fact, that evening, it was cold and wet, and over a hundred people turned up in the darkness. I supplied them with knives and forks and served them a hot meal. What they filmed was just me doing my work really. On other occasions, it was me praying with someone who'd just lost their daughter, Father Alex speaking from his heart, and the two of us explaining what we were doing and why. You see, our hope for the piece they were filming was that it would include my van with its 'Church on the Street' and cross on the side, and the two of us in dog collars. We felt that that would be as strong a Christian message as the BBC were likely to broadcast, and we did want a Christian message.

But we got far more.

The day came when the item went out. It was broadcast on the six o'clock and the ten o'clock national news. And what we thought was our everyday work truly horrified those viewing. Our tears became the tears of a nation. My phone rang non-stop. My email address almost got burnt out. It turned out millions and millions of people had watched the programme – there were all these comments, all these people trying to contact us.

Then an absolutely miraculous thing happened. Money started to appear in our bank account. We had a tiny little website with a donate button and it almost exploded overnight with the funds that were being put through it. Nevertheless, it was strapped up and held together well enough to just about manage.

The thing is, we hadn't asked anybody for anything. I spoke to Father Alex and we both got kind of lost in what was happening. I'd get letters and cards through the post with people wanting to support the ministry and saying they were praying for us. There were old ladies sending two or three pounds, and children offering their pocket money to people they'd seen on TV.

If I didn't have any humility before, I certainly had it afterwards. The power of that piece was enormous. It's become a piece of history, a chronicle of the pandemic and the poverty people found themselves in.

With the donations we received, we managed to secure a building – the building that now is Church on the Street headquarters. Having this wonderful home – and enough money to create a safe space for the future – allows us to do the work we now do. I'll forever be grateful to the three people who produced, edited and directed that film. They'd become our friends. We shared something very painful and very special together, and through that sharing hope was born! When everything was still shut and locked down, we managed to provide the town with a place it so needed.

I spoke to Ed when things were beginning to calm down a little. In fact, he was anxious to check up on me and Father Alex – he wanted to be sure we were all right. I believed in this man then. We weren't just a news item for him. There was much more involved than that. I believe he would have scrapped the film if he'd thought it would affect us in a negative way. Ed seemed to care.

I met him for a coffee on my own and he said, 'Mick, just tell me about your life.'

So I did.

After ten minutes of relating the story I've written in this book, a swear word came out of his mouth. The second word was 'hell'!

I said, 'That's right, Ed; that's what my life's been like.'

'Can I write a little piece about it just for our website, Mick?'

I sat and thought about it for a moment and asked what good did he think it would do?

'Well, it will show people that God's changed your life.'

I just nodded. Yeah.

So Ed wrote a short two-thousand-word piece about me. And that's when the fireworks really started. People from all over the world were contacting me: churches, Christian organizations, secular organizations. The letters, the donations, the cries for help became so overwhelming, I couldn't possibly respond to them all. There were offers for books and even for films – most of which I refused because I'm not really a movie star! I'm just a broken person who's trying to show other people where the river is so they can have a drink, I guess. The little bit of writing that went on the website opened a door, and I either walked through it or I didn't. But I knew once I'd walked through there'd be no going back.

I stepped forward . . . into the next chapter.

* * *

A few months later, Ed phoned again and asked me what I thought was happening. My heart was really, really heavy. I was doing so many funerals – in fact, I was almost doing one funeral a day. It was getting ridiculous. The undertakers were having to hire hearses just to keep up with the demand. In that January period, I was seeing death like I'd never seen it before.

Ed asked, 'Is it all COVID deaths, Mick?'

And I said, 'No – it's just death. And it's linked to poverty.'

'I'm coming up to see you.'

When he arrived, he asked me some questions and I answered as well as I could.

'Would you allow us to do a film about the funerals and the death and the other things you're seeing?'

I trusted Ed. I felt confident that if the people around me who would feature in the film were happy enough, then I'd be happy enough. I felt this was a story that needed telling. You see, there were people dying and their loved ones couldn't access grants and loans to bury them. They were getting pauper's funerals or, more usually, no funeral at all. Their bodies were simply being burnt. It seemed all wrong to me. Due to the donations resulting from the BBC film, I was in a position to pay for those funerals. And I could do the funerals myself and not charge.

Ed and the team filmed me with two families who were grieving. One had lost a beautiful young woman, twenty-eight or twenty-nine years old, who had died and left behind a son, little Deacon. Her mother was so shattered and lost, and her grandmother just the same. I was able to do the funeral and the BBC followed it. Afterwards, they asked Deacon if there was anything he wanted to say.

And his words – to this day – almost break my heart: 'I just want me mum back. I'm only ten. I shouldn't have to go through this.'

I remember him following the coffin with Grace in it. I remember hearing that primeval scream from her mother, which echoed my own mum's so long ago. I looked at Deacon and I saw myself. I loved these people. Taking that funeral was one of the most difficult things I've ever done. But I did it.

And then there was Janet, whose husband had died in hospital. She didn't have the money for the funeral, and the hospital was going to 'take care' of the body. So we provided a kind of memorial service, just so she could have *something*.

It turned out that if you lived in Burnley that January, you were sixty per cent more likely to die than if you lived anywhere else in the country. An appalling statistic. Poverty and death indistinguishable. This is something that has spoken to me over the years: the injustice of poverty. I won't accept it. I will *not* accept it. Till my dying breath, I'll stand up against poverty, because poverty is failing to offer equal access to the things everyone should have. If you have equal access, you're no longer poor. And all the poor require is the same access that you and I may have. But they don't. Society is organized in such a way that it puts a foot on the throat of the poor and holds them down. But in Christ Jesus, that injustice is reversed.

The New Testament and the Old Testament are full of passages that cry out – *scream* out – against anyone or anything that oppresses the poor. *I pray that all churches, around the world, grasp that message!* The reality of helping the poor is that it isn't only about prayer; it's also about deeds of the heart, in the name of Jesus Christ. We're called to feed and serve and love and care for those in need, and it's about time we started doing it more.

That piece, though heart-breaking, became so redemptive that only a year or so later a chance meeting brought Deacon and the future king of England together in the most unlikely of ways . . .

For now, the ministry of Church on the Street was growing strongly, and I was becoming a face on TV and a voice on the radio as I tried to speak truth into different situations and to share the love of God. The new building was set up so it might serve in many different ways. If you can, imagine if monasteries were invented tomorrow – what would a twenty-first-century monastery be like? Well, I guess it would be independent. It would have health facilities, mental health facilities and drug facilities; it would help people into housing and out of debt; it would feed people, wash people, wrap bandages around their sores . . . That's what Church on the Street was aiming to provide.

And right through the centre of it all was the church itself. Our Sunday services looked a little bit different. They had between 150 and 200 broken people who gathered and became whole together. We were honest in our poverty and we shared what we had with one another. We had hope, for the present and for the future. We were not trapped.

* * *

I began to notice there was a new pandemic: many more people were developing serious mental health issues or taking their own lives. I'd have people coming to see me, and after I'd prayed with them or tried to support them, I'd ring mental health services and nothing would happen.

They'd go away and die.

I began to feel incensed by the injustice of it . . . You know that anger that wells up inside you and twists and turns in the pit of your stomach? I wanted to shout and bellow out loud. And I knew something had to be done.

Once again, I contacted my old friend Ed. He and Phil came to see me and we spoke about the ministry and how things had grown, and what we were doing now. There were over a thousand people a week coming through the church to get help and support. The need was great, but the mental health issues in particular were colossal.

Ed asked me what I'd like to see, so I repeated my refrain about equal access. I wanted these guys, who were desperate, lost and wanting to die, to have access to good mental health treatment. And it just wasn't being offered. We'd asked the mental health teams to come in and they wouldn't. We tried to access them by phone but no one would get back to us.

And I'm ashamed and really sad to say this, but the bodies were piling up. Young people. Lost.

So the BBC did a feature on mental health. As before, they followed me in my everyday ministry and it was almost supernatural what happened as they were filming – just the right people would turn up at the right time. They saw the extremes of behaviour exhibited by people with very poor mental health; they documented the lack of access and the lack of support.

The film had such a colossal impact, it led to the NHS contacting me and offering support. In line with our vision, we've been able to set up a mental health team with workers coming in. We have trauma counsellors. We have a medical room that treats people who have abscesses in their legs and groins, wounds and DVTs in their legs, and skin falling off their arms. We have treatment teams who help people with hep C. The local housing authority comes to offer aid to rough sleepers. We have drug and alcohol services who try to get people back on the right track and into services. We have rehab once a week. We have supportive groups run by outside organizations who come just to talk and chat. We have groups for the families and loved ones of addicts and alcoholics. We feed people hot food every day, seven days a week. We have a foodbank. We have a clothes bank. We have showers that are free to access. We help people with their gas and electricity bills. We pay for people's funerals. We help people with their benefit claims.

That is Church on the Street.

That is a twenty-first-century monastery.

That is how a Christian community is built.

15
THE PHONE CALL

IT WAS A COLD, WET MORNING and there was rain pattering on the window as I sat in my office at Church on the Street. I watched a lady running past with an umbrella – hanging on to it really! Strong gusts were lifting the sections between the spokes, this way and that, almost as if they were dancing like leaves in the wind.

The dull weather meant the streetlamps were still on, and the wet stone flags of the pavement glowed with reflected light. Beauty in the ordinary always makes me wonder about the majesty of God. It doesn't matter if you're in the city centre, or a town or a village, God is the extraordinary *in* the ordinary. We only need to open our eyes to see it, to breathe it in . . .

The phone rang. I look down and see it's the dreaded 'private number'. There's virtually zero possibility of me answering a call from a private number – my thinking's always been: 'If you can't tell me who you are, I don't really want to talk to you.' But it's ringing and ringing and, in a one-in-a-million chance, I answer it. *Very cautiously.* My hand's hovering over the button that ends the call.

'Hello, is that Pastor Mick?'

The voice sounds educated. Perfectly pronounced vowels. My first thought is that it's a detective or maybe even a police sergeant. 'Hello.'

'It's Kensington Palace.'

I picked up a pen and speed wrote 'Kensington Palace', because I thought I knew what it was, but I wasn't entirely sure . . .

It turned out they wanted to invite me to a meeting on Zoom with regard to a visit. And that was all the information I was given. Of course I accepted. But I was to keep it to myself, which was quite difficult really, because after we'd arranged a time and I put the phone down, I googled Kensington Palace and it wasn't actually a football team! No, it was the office of the royals!

I couldn't help laughing. I thought about my life and where I'd come from, and what I'd done and what I'd been. And I prayed, 'Lord, you must be joking! We're not going to have a royal come to see us here . . . are we?' Surely that would be the biggest miracle of all.

Just then there's a knock on the door and one of the guys who works with us pops his head in to ask if I want a coffee.

'Yeah!'

'What's up?' he says.

'Nothing . . . why?'

'You've got a big smile on your face.'

'Why? Is that unusual?'

'Well, it is for you, Mick, yeah!'

We both laugh together.

'No, nothing, nothing.' I'm sworn to secrecy.

He comes back with my coffee and I feel as if I'm going to explode, I'm so desperate to tell him what's happened.

But I can't.

* * *

When the time came for the Zoom meeting, I went into a different room and locked myself in. I could see all these different faces with little borders and I couldn't help wondering about how they were brought up and what had happened in their lives. I didn't feel they were privileged and I wasn't. I just felt really interested, you know? What does it take to work at Kensington Palace? What do you have to be or not be? Do you work for the government, even? I kind of imagined a James Bond-type character doing the bodyguarding . . . there were all sort of thoughts wandering through my mind as I gazed at those square faces in square borders on a square screen.

All flat though. And not really real. There, but hundreds of miles away. Yet a crystal-clear connection and a conversation in which they were all proposing something so exciting I could only just contain myself.

The Duke and Duchess of Cambridge wanted to come and see us at Church on the Street. They were particularly interested in meeting me! And they were exceptionally interested in the work we did.

I remember sitting there trying to work out who the Duke and Duchess of Cambridge are! And then it came to me: it's Prince William! This geezer's going to be the king one day! And his missus, that tall lass, she's going to be the queen. The meeting seemed to fade into the background as I started to imagine people with crowns on, and royal gowns and all sorts of things . . . I had to shake my head and bring myself back down to earth and into the conversation.

I asked, 'Is this something that will happen in twelve months' time or six months' time?' I was thinking these things take a lot of preparation.

'No, no, no – it will be in two weeks.'

'So you're telling me that in two weeks' time, the future king and queen of England are going to be coming up to Burnley, popping in to have a cup of tea *with me*, and to take a look round at the work we're doing?'

'That's right, Pastor Mick, yeah.'

Nice one!

I didn't know which was more surprising – me being about to meet the future king and queen, or the conversation I'd had with an angel. The two were quite similar and equally impossible . . . but real.

A recce was organized, and a few days later the full team arrived from London to consult with us. When the three security men and one security lady came into the main office, it was clear to me they were carrying guns. I could tell by the way they stood in the room, by *how* they stood in the room, by how quiet they were. They wandered round the building and checked all the exits while we made conversation with the rest of the team. Of course, I'd had to tell some of our staff about the visit, although we did as much as we could to keep things under wraps. Nothing could get out to the general public: it was coming towards the end of the lockdown period, but there was still a lot of uncertainty and this would be the first official engagement the Duke and Duchess had undertaken for quite some time.

And it was all arranged. We had an itinerary. I'd been thinking to myself that they'd come and spend ten or fifteen minutes with us, shake hands, have some pictures taken and off they'd go. But no. It soon became apparent they wanted to stay for an hour and a half.

More and more remarkable. I kept thinking, *This is not going to happen. It'll just be called off. This is not real – it'll never come to pass.*

When I'd told Sarah the news, we laughed. I said, 'You know, I'm the kind of man they wouldn't let within two hundred miles of somebody from the royal family, yet they're coming to see us. It's remarkable.'

'It is remarkable, Mick,' she said. 'What a blessing from God!'

And I think that's what it was. It really was a blessing from God.

The security team spoke to me and said if I could vouch for everybody who was going to be in the building, that would be good enough for them. The trust that people were putting in me! They were trusting me in the company of the future king and queen. I felt humbled and blessed. I wasn't too afraid, though there was a dancing feeling in my stomach – a mixture of excitement and not knowing . . .

Soon the dots were dotted, the ticks were ticked, and within two weeks we were going to have some very special visitors. So we had to invite some special people to speak to them. Everybody I know is special, but I had in mind Deacon, whose mother we'd buried. He did something to me, that boy. He had something about him. I felt he could break the mould and the pattern of life here and maybe even break out of Burnley. I'd always felt that for him. He was just a little lad, and those words of his had impacted me, deep down inside: 'I just want me mum back. I'm only ten. I shouldn't have to go through this.'

If anyone deserved to meet a king – and a queen – it was him.

So I invited Deacon and his great-grandma. They were the first two on the list. And, of course, all the staff and some of the service users who come in. I hate using the term 'service users' because they're just friends, but sometimes when you write things down you need a distinguishing phrase.

We didn't go mad, you know, making everything spick and span and polished. We had a bit of a flick round, because we're pretty respectful, but on the day of the visit we stayed open until two o'clock before we had to shut the building down.

It's about ten to three. We've got TV and radio crews milling around, newspaper and magazine reporters . . . We'd asked if it would be okay not to have too many dignitaries attending, because we wanted the focus to be on the work we're doing rather than anything else, and that was honoured.

Then whispers: 'They're here! They're here!'

There was the sound of the front door opening. We're one flight up, and I could hear footsteps – a clippety-clop, a little shuffle. Obviously they weren't going to be climbing the stairs really slowly, hanging on to the rail – they're fit and active people! So they walked up at pace. They were eager. And then they were here!

Prince William put his hand out, and the words that came out of his mouth almost knocked me off my feet. This tall young man, the future king of England, said, 'Pastor Mick! The main man!'

As I shook hands with him and then with his beautiful wife, I said, 'Thank you. Thank you for coming. Thank you for honouring us because, you know, your visit here's going to definitely help us. Maybe people will support us more, and . . .'

It was amazing.

I'd a little tour set up, and I showed them round. I introduced them to my wife and explained she does people's nails in the church. Some of those who come in are really, really struggling, and when they sit opposite Sarah at the table, she touches their hands and paints their nails and listens and has a conversation. It's an amazing ministry that unlocks so many dark souls and lets light in.

And Sarah was just Sarah! She was having a laugh and talking to both of them. They were such nice people.

We'd three tables set up, and at the first we introduced them to Deacon and his great-grandmother. She was so pleased, so proud. The smile on her face! Deacon was a little bit reserved and quiet, but we hadn't been able to tell him who was coming.

I said, 'What's up, Deacon?'

'Oh, I thought it were going to be, like, David Beckham or some other footballer.'

I said, 'Oh, don't worry about it; it's all right.' I didn't know if he was disappointed or not!

But the Prince just went straight into conversation with him. And I watched an amazing thing happen. 'How do you know Pastor Mick?'

'Well, he helped us when me mum died.'

'Wow. When did she die, Deacon?'

'Just a year ago.'

I feel what I'm about to describe is one of the most special moments I've ever seen.

Prince William leant a little closer to Deacon and said, 'You know, Deacon, I lost my mum when I was fifteen. Don't *ever* stop talking about her! Don't hide away. Keep her memory alive.'

And in that moment, they bonded. They *knew* each other! They'd experienced the same pain. I saw Deacon's face change. It became lighter and his eyes opened wider. And the Duchess was so beautiful. Her smile and charm as she looked at this young boy . . . it melted people's hearts.

Deacon's great-grandma wiped a tear away.

The Prince noticed that Deacon was wearing a football shirt, a goalkeeper's shirt, a *Burnley* goalkeeper's shirt! And on the back it said 'Nick Pope'. He knew everything about football – well, maybe not that much; he's an Aston Villa fan! But, you know, you have to forgive that!

And he talked to Deacon about football, about the players, and then he said, 'Would you like to meet Nick Pope?'

The smile that came across Deacon's face. It was like the edges of his lips were on string and someone had pulled both sides up as high as they could. I've never seen a bigger smile. 'Yeah!'

'Well, I'm the chairman of the FA, so really I'm his boss! I'll see what I can do.'

Miraculous. Absolutely miraculous.

We moved on to the next table, where Anthony was sitting with his mum and dad. He told his story of change. He came to Church on the Street to steal coffee from the food parcels to buy drugs. Now he works for us. He's clean, he's sober and he no longer attends court proceedings or lives in prison cells. He's a productive member of society.

I remember the Prince turned to him and said, 'We've come here for you, Anthony, to talk to people like you. It's you that's important, not us.'

And I knew he meant it.

Anthony was moved to tears. I could feel my eyes welling up a little too. The Prince stood up and asked Anthony if he could have a photograph with him. You see, that's what they did! They let us take photographs. They were down-to-earth people. They cared. And they were just so interested.

I felt moved in my heart to ask if I could pray for them. And they agreed: 'Yes, of course.' So we moved over to the corner of the room and bowed our heads, and I let the words spill out of my mouth. I prayed protection over them. I prayed that God would guide them in all they needed to do. I prayed for them as the future hope of our nation, with so much riding on who and what they are, and how they conduct and handle themselves. Then I wrapped it all up with, 'God bless you.'

As they walked towards the reception area to leave, they passed one of our volunteers, who had just had a little baby, Anastasia. And the Duchess was straight in! She cuddled the baby, and the press loved it. Especially when the Duke, with a wry smile on his face, said, 'Don't be getting any ideas!' Such laughter filled the room.

As the door opened at the bottom of the stairs, there was a great cheer. A huge crowd had gathered outside. And that night, on the *BBC News at Six*, was Church on the Street, this strange vicar called Pastor Mick, and the Duke and Duchess of Cambridge.

What a conversation!

What an unlikely existence I've lived!

The pictures of the Duchess with little Anastasia went viral, and images of the conversation and the prayer we'd shared appeared in magazines and were printed widely, including in America, China and Japan.

Within a few days, there was a phone call from Kensington Palace. It was arranged that Deacon and his family and I would go to Burnley Football Club, to be guests in the Directors' Box and enjoy a meal, and Deacon would get to meet the players, including – very specially! – Nick Pope.

And it happened, you know? It really did happen. We went to the football match and that little lad met his hero. Nick gave him his shirt and signed it; he gave him his goalkeeper's gloves and signed them; and he took Deacon on to the pitch and into the goal area and talked with him, and there was such genuineness and care in it all.

The Prince was true to his word. Deacon had the day of his life. And the story touched hearts around the world.

Deacon's problems began to melt away. He's become so much more talkative, and it feels as if the healing process is really kicking in.

* * *

As I've written this book, I've related stories of my drug addiction, my recovery, my becoming a Christian, my setting up Church on the Street . . . and it's become clear to me that my life has been one of extremes.

But one thing I can see running right through the middle of it is Jesus Christ, my Lord and Saviour.

RESOURCES AND FURTHER INFORMATION

I hope you've enjoyed reading *Blown Away*. If you've been touched by anything in the book, please do contact me. You'll find information on how to do this below, along with resources to use if you'd like. (Additional press coverage may be accessed online.)

Pastor Mick's contact details

Email: pastormick@cots-ministries.co.uk
Twitter: https://twitter.com/pastorfleming?lang=en
Facebook: https://www.facebook.com/mick.fleming.75

For resources to use with this book

www.cots-ministries.co.uk
Church on the Street (COTS) has developed a set of resources to accompany *Blown Away*. These can be accessed digitally or in print form, and include videos from Mick. The resources will expand, in an authentic way, on the elements of change Mick experienced, pulling out the patterns that led directly to Christ and teaching people how to apply these practically. Suitable for churches, groups and individuals, the resources were launched as part of a membership programme in September 2022, coinciding with the publication of *Blown Away*.

TV and radio coverage

BBC News

Pastor Mick: Duke and Duchess show support for Burnley charity (20.1.22)
www.bbc.co.uk/news/uk-england-lancashire-60070614

Prince William and Kate meet Burnley's Pastor Mick (20.1.22)
www.bbc.co.uk/news/av/uk-60062262

The Cost of Covid: A Year on the Frontline (11.12.21)
www.bbc.co.uk/iplayer/episode/m0012kd4/the-cost-of-covid
-a-year-on-the-frontline

'I don't want to live, my mental health's that bad' (25.10.21)
www.bbc.co.uk/news/av/uk-59044611

Burnley's Pastor Mick: 'If I lock this door, he dies' (17.12.21)
www.bbc.co.uk/news/uk-59651954

Burnley's Pastor Mick – from dangerous drug dealer to lifesaver
(18.12.20)
www.bbc.co.uk/news/stories-55273677

BBC *Songs of Praise*
Pendle Radicals: Burnley's Pastor Mick (12.9.21)
www.bbc.co.uk/programmes/m000zp4l (*Songs of Praise*)

GB TV
Pastor Mick Fleming exclusively tells *GB News* about the rising
cost of living in Burnley (4.2.22)
www.youtube.com/watch?v=yg5-ggvBN7o

ZDF (Germany's national public television broadcaster)
New ZDF documentary *Poor Kingdom* (29.5.22)
www.zdf.de/nachrichten/heute-journal/neue-zdf-doku-armes
-koenigreich-102.html

Premier Radio
A Mucky Business with Tim Farron: BBC featured Pastor Mick
Fleming: a call to weep with the poor (8.2.22)
www.premierchristianradio.com/Shows/Weekday/A-Mucky
-Business-with-Tim-Farron/Podcast/BBC-featured-Pastor-Mick
-Fleming-a-call-to-weep-with-the-poor

Press coverage

The Guardian

'We've been hammered': on the breadline in Burnley (29.12.21)
www.theguardian.com/society/2021/oct/24/weve-been
-hammered-on-the-breadline-in-burnley-covid-universal-credit

Helping the helpers: it's time to support those who hold Britain's communities together (29.12.21)
www.theguardian.com/commentisfree/2021/dec/29/helping
-helpers-britain-communities-vulnerable-people-guardian
-video

From dealing drugs to delivering food: Pastor Mick on Burnley's Covid crisis – video report (25.2.21)
www.theguardian.com/uk-news/video/2021/feb/25/from
-dealing-drugs-to-delivering-food-pastor-mick-on-burnleys
-covid-crisis-video-report

Original *Observer* photography: Pastor Mick Fleming and Father Alex Frost, photographed at St Matthew's Church in Burnley (2.1.21)
www.theguardian.com/artanddesign/gallery/2021/jan/02
/original-observer-photography?page=with%3Aimg-11

Destitution is rising fast due to Covid and flaws in the benefit system (9.12.20)
www.theguardian.com/society/2020/dec/09/destitution-is-rising
-fast-due-to-covid-and-flaws-in-the-benefit-system

Exploitation of the poor borders on evil, say clerics driven to tears by debt crisis (5.12.20)
www.theguardian.com/money/2020/dec/05/exploitation-of-the
-poor-borders-on-evil-say-clerics-driven-to-tears-by-debt
-crisis

The Telegraph

Prince William sets up 'life-changing' meeting between grieving boy and his footballing hero after bonding over losing their mothers (15.2.22)

www.telegraph.co.uk/royal-family/2022/02/15/prince-william -sets-life-changing-meeting-grieving-boy-footballing/

The Times

Churches have the networks to help poor in time of need (6.12.20)

www.thetimes.co.uk/article/churches-have-the-networks-to -help-poor-in-time-of-need-50jzklmld

The Daily Mail

Pastor who was a violent drug dealer before setting up a charity for the disadvantaged and homeless meets the Duke and Duchess of Cambridge during visit to Lancashire (20.1.22)

www.dailymail.co.uk/femail/article-10424527/Pastor-drug -dealer-meets-Duke-Duchess-Cambridge.html

The Independent

Happy List 2021: *The Independent* celebrates 50 inspirational people driving positive change in Britain: Michael Fleming

www.independent.co.uk/happylist/happy-list-2021-inspirational -individuals-b1899386.html

The Lancashire Telegraph

Burnley gangster turned pastor shortlisted for Brave Britons (13.7.22)

www.lancashiretelegraph.co.uk/news/20275926.burnley -gangster-turned-pastor-shortlisted-brave-britons-2022-charity -champion/

Pastor to open new café where most vulnerable eat free (6.5.22)
www.lancashiretelegraph.co.uk/news/20119833.barnoldswick -pastor-open-new-cafe-vulnerable-eat-free/

Burnley ex-gangster turned pastor writes autobiography (7.4.22)
www.lancashiretelegraph.co.uk/news/20052009.burnley-ex -gangster-turned-pastor-writes-autobiography/

Food bank use has doubled in last four months, according to pastor (23.3.22)
www.lancashiretelegraph.co.uk/news/national/uk-today /20013461.food-bank-use-doubled-last-four-months-according -pastor/

Pastor appears on *GB News* to discuss cost of living crisis in East Lancs town (15.2.22)
www.lancashiretelegraph.co.uk/news/19925464.burnley-pastor -appears-gb-news-discuss-cost-living-crisis/

William and Kate make new friends with 'Alfie' and hail the work of Burnley Church volunteers (20.1.22)
www.lancashiretelegraph.co.uk/news/19863457.william-kate -make-new-friends-alfie-hail-work-burnley-church-volunteers/

Christmas charity single released to help Burnley community (23.12.21)
www.lancashiretelegraph.co.uk/news/19806519.christmas -charity-single-released-help-burnley-community-church/

Burnley ex-gangster turned pastor features on *Songs of Praise* (13.9.21)
www.lancashiretelegraph.co.uk/news/19577611.burnley-ex -gangster-turned-pastor-features-songs-praise/

The *Church Times*
Press: *Mail* cares more for Dibley than for Burnley (11.12.20)
www.churchtimes.co.uk/articles/2020/11-december/comment /columnists/press-mail-cares-more-for-dibley-than-for-burnley

Hello!

Kate Middleton and Prince William meet therapy puppy at Lancashire hospital (see second part of article) (20.1.22)
www.hellomagazine.com/royalty/gallery/20220120131270/kate -middleton-prince-william-meet-therapy-puppy-lancashire/1/

The *New York Times*

Mick features twice in the Britain section of this article (undated)
www.nytimes.com/interactive/2021/04/29/magazine/life -expectancy-australia-britain-malawi.html

Church on the Street

An interview with Mick Fleming (22.5.20)
https://nazarene.ac.uk/combating-social-injustice-ntc-alumnus -pastor-mick-fleming/

New Life Publishing

Hitman who got another shot at life! (11.5.21)
www.newlifepublishing.co.uk/articles/hitman-who-got-another -shot-at-life/

The *Global Herald*

Pastor Mick Fleming exclusively tells *GB News* about the rising cost of living in Burnley (4.2.22)
https://theglobalherald.com/news/pastor-mick-fleming -exclusively-tells-gb-news-about-the-rising-cost-of-living-in-burnley/

Awards

2021 Sandford St Martin Trustees' Awards: Trustees' Content Award – Burnley Crisis
https://sandfordawards.org.uk/2021-trustees-awards/

The Orwell Prize for Exposing Britain's Social Evils 2022: The Cost of Covid – Burnley Crisis by Ed Thomas (*BBC News*)
www.orwellfoundation.com/the-orwell-foundation/news-events /news-events/news/the-orwell-prizes-2022-winners/